100
Bible Stories
for Children

100
Bible Stories
for Children

Retold by Jackie Andrews
Illustrated by Val Biro

Testament Books
New York

This 2005 edition is published by Testament Books, an imprint of Random House Value Publishing,
a division of Random House, Inc., New York by arrangement with
Award Publications Limited, London.

Random House
New York • Toronto • London • Sydney • Auckland
www.randomhouse.com

Printed and bound in Malaysia

A catalog record for this title is available from the Library of Congress.

ISBN 0-517-22586-7

10 9 8 7 6 5 4 3 2 1

Contents

The Old Testament

The New Testament

The Old Testament

In the beginning

Many years ago, there was just God. He made
everything. At first there was just water and empty
darkness.

Then God made light. He divided light from dark
and called the light "day" and the darkness "night".

Then God made the sky and the mighty heavens.

God looked at all he had made and was pleased
with it.

Then God made dry land rise up out of the water.
God called the land "earth" and the water "sea". He
made plants and trees to cover the earth.

Next, God put lights in the sky: the sun to brighten

the day and the shining moon and stars to light up
the night.

Then God made all kinds of animals and birds to live
on the earth and fill the skies, and fish to fill the seas.

God looked at all these things and was pleased with
them.

Then God made men and women to live on the
earth. He made them just like himself, to be his friends.
God blessed the people he had made and told them to
have families and fill the earth, and to take care of all the
plants and animals.

When God had finished making heaven and earth, he
had a rest. He looked down from heaven on everything
he had created, and saw that it was all very good indeed.

The first mother and father

When God made the dry land rise up out of the water, nothing could live there at first. So God made streams to flow from the ground and water the land. The dry earth turned to mud, which God took and formed into the figure of a man. Then he breathed into the figure and gave it life. The name of this first living person was Adam.

God planted a beautiful garden for Adam, filled with trees and flowers. In the centre of this Garden of Eden grew the tree of the knowledge of good and evil. God told Adam that he could eat any of the fruits of the trees, except those growing on the tree of knowledge.

After a while, God saw that Adam needed a friend and helper. He shaped all the wild animals and birds from the soil, but none of these was a suitable companion for Adam. So God made Adam fall into a deep sleep, and took a rib bone from him. Then he made a woman out of the rib bone and brought her to Adam. Adam called her Eve, and loved her dearly. And Adam and Eve were the father and mother of all people on earth.

The Fall

O f all the creatures that God made, the serpent was the most cunning. It crept up to Eve and asked her if it was true they weren't supposed to eat the fruit from any of the trees in this garden.

"We may eat the fruit of any of the trees," said Eve, "but not that of the tree in the middle of the garden. We may not touch it, or we will die."

The snake told her that it was not true. The fruit would give them wonderful knowledge. They would be like gods.

So Eve picked some of the fruit and ate it. Then she took some to Adam and gave it to him to eat. Immediately, their eyes opened and they realised that they were naked. So they sewed together some fig leaves to cover themselves.

Just then, they heard God walking in the garden. Adam and Eve hid among the trees because they were ashamed. God asked them both what they had done. Adam said, "It was the woman's fault: she gave me the fruit!"

And Eve said, "It was the serpent: he told me to eat it!"

God was very angry. Because they had disobeyed him, God sent Adam and Eve out of the Garden of Eden for ever. From then on, Adam would have to work and find his own food to live. Life would not be easy any longer.

And God told the snake, "You are the most cursed of all creatures. You and the woman will always be enemies, and one day her child will crush your head and you will strike his heel!"

Cain and Abel

Adam and Eve eventually had two sons. The oldest was Cain, the other was Abel. Abel became a shepherd looking after flocks of sheep, while Cain worked on the land, growing crops for food.

After a time, Cain brought some of his produce as an offering to God. Abel brought an offering of the best lambs from his flocks. God was pleased with Abel and his offering, but he did not accept Cain or his gifts.

Cain was angry and disappointed. He became very jealous of Abel.

God warned Cain to be careful: "Sin is crouching at your door like a wild animal ready to pounce!" He meant the evil feelings lurking inside Cain's heart.

But Cain took no notice. Instead, Cain invited Abel to go for a walk in the countryside with him. As soon as they reached a lonely place, Cain attacked his brother and killed him.

"Where is your brother?" asked God, when Cain returned.

Cain pretended not to know. "I can't be expected to look after him!" he said.

"What have you done?" said God. "I can hear your brother's blood crying out to me from the ground. From now on, the ground will never give you any food. You will be a restless wanderer for the rest of your life."

Cain begged God not to give him such a harsh punishment. If he had to leave God's presence and wander the earth, his life would be in great danger. So God put a special mark on Cain to make sure that no one would harm him. Cain left and went to live in a land east of Eden.

Noah and his ark

G od had created Adam and Eve so that their
descendants would fill the earth. He wanted them
to be kind and loving to each other.

Instead, God saw that there was a great deal of
wickedness in their hearts, and it made him very sad.

"I shall rid the earth of all its people, as well as all the
animals, plants, creeping things and birds of the heavens,
for I am sorry I created them."

But there was one man who pleased God, and that
was Noah, who was always his loyal servant. God

explained to Noah what he had decided to do: "I am going to cause a great flood to destroy all life. I want you to make an ark out of strong wood. Cover it with pitch to make it waterproof. Then take your family into the ark, along with two of every kind of animal. In this way, I will be able to start afresh."

Noah did just as God had told him. He made his ark strong and safe, and then he filled it with his entire family, and a pair of every kind of bird and animal. Then God shut the door and the storms came.

The sign of the rainbow

The rain fell for forty days. First the waters covered the land and filled the valleys. Then they covered the hills. Finally they covered the mountains. Every living thing was drowned. But Noah and his family were safe in the ark with all the animals, just as God had planned.

Eventually it stopped raining, but it was still a long time before the waters started to go down. After two months, Noah sent out first a raven and then a dove to look for signs of dry land, but there was nothing. Then he sent out the dove again, and this time it came back with an olive leaf in its beak. Now Noah knew that the earth was becoming dry again.

Noah left the ark on dry land and immediately he made an altar to worship God and give thanks for their safety.

God blessed Noah and his sons: "Fill the earth with children," he told them. "Look after the animals and birds, trees and plants. Follow my ways and I will always be your God."

Then he made a solemn promise to Noah. "Never again will a flood destroy all living creatures, or the earth be covered in water. There will be time to sow seed and harvest crops; cold and heat, summer and winter, day and night. I will put my rainbow in the heavens as a sign of my promise to you and your children and every living creature in the world."

The tower of Babel

Many years had passed and Noah's descendants gradually spread over the land. Eventually some settled in the land of Shinar.

In those days everyone in the world spoke the same language and used the same words. The people of Shinar decided to build themselves a fine city out of brick, with a tall tower that would be the highest in the world and reach right up to the heavens. They thought this would make them all famous and powerful: the envy of every other nation! No longer would they be weak, and scattered over the countryside.

While they were still making bricks and building, God came down to see what they were doing. The sight

of their city, with its strong walls and its tower reaching
up to the sky, made him sad. These people, he saw, were
full of pride and selfish ambition. Once their city was
built, there would be no end to their greedy scheming;
nothing would stop them.

So God confused their language and the words they
spoke, so that they were all unable to understand each
other. At once the building came to a stop and the tower
of Babel – which took its name from the babble of
sounds that everyone made – was never completed. The
people left the Shinar valley and scattered in many
different directions once more.

The story of Abraham

Abraham was a rich man who lived in the city of Ur, in Mesopotamia. He was devoted to God and had been obedient to him all his life. When Abraham was seventy-five years old, God called him and said: "Leave your home and go to the new land I shall show you. I will be your God and will bless you and your family."

Abraham trusted God. He took his wife, Sarah, his nephew, Lot, their servants, sheep and goats and everything they owned, and set off in search of the land of Canaan, stopping only whenever they found water for their animals.

Abraham continued travelling through Canaan until he reached the holy place of Shechem. There, God appeared to him again. "Look all around you. I am going to give this land to you and your descendants."

From Shechem, Abraham travelled on towards the mountains. Again, God appeared to him. "Look up at the stars," he said to Abraham. "Can you count them? No, there are too many. I promise you that one day your descendants will be just as numerous!"

Now Abraham trusted God, but he was worried because he and Sarah had no children. His wife was now too old to have them. But nothing was impossible to God. Just as he had promised, Sarah gave birth to a little boy and they called him Isaac. Now Abraham could indeed be the father of many people.

Sodom and Gomorrah

While Abraham settled in Canaan, his nephew Lot took his family and went to live in Jordan, in the city of Sodom.

Unfortunately, Sodom and its neighbouring city, Gomorrah, were full of wicked people who did terrible things.

God told Abraham that because the people were so wicked, he was going to have to destroy both cities. It was the only way to get rid of such evil.

But Abraham thought about his nephew, Lot, and did not want Sodom to be destroyed.

"Would you really want to destroy innocent people as well?" he asked the Lord God. "Supposing there are fifty good people in the city, wouldn't you want to spare the place for their sake?"

"If I find fifty good people in Sodom, then I shall not destroy it," said the Lord God.

Abraham spoke up again, apologising for being so bold. "Suppose there were only ten good people in the city, Lord? Would you still destroy it?"

"No, if there are ten good people, I shall not do it."

But God knew that the only good people living in Sodom were Lot and his family. He had sent his angels to Lot to warn him to escape from the city.

By early morning the earth shook. Fire and sulphur rained down on Sodom and Gomorrah, destroying them completely. Lot and his daughters ran safely away, but Lot's wife turned back to take a last look at her home, and was turned into a pillar of salt.

Abraham and Isaac

After a few years had passed, God tested Abraham to see if he was still faithful to him.

"Abraham!" he called. "Take your son Isaac, whom you love so much, and offer him as a sacrifice on the mountain I shall show you."

Early next day, Abraham saddled up his donkey. He chopped some wood to make a fire for the sacrifice and gave the bundle to Isaac to carry. Then, together with two servants, they set off on their journey.

On the third day Abraham knew they had reached the right place. He told the servants to stay at their camp. Then he and Isaac continued up the mountain, with Isaac carrying the wood and Abraham carrying the container of hot coals for the fire.

After a while, Isaac turned to Abraham and asked him: "Father, we have the fire and the wood for the sacrifice, but where is the lamb?"

"My son," said Abraham, "God himself will provide the lamb."

Abraham built an altar and arranged the wood around it. Then he tied Isaac's hands and feet and lay him on the altar, on top of the wood. He then took up his knife and stretched out his hand to kill his son.

But an angel from God stopped him. "Abraham!" he said. "Do not harm the boy. God knows that you are indeed faithful to him, and that you would do anything for him, even sacrifice your son."

Abraham looked up and saw a ram stuck in the bushes nearby. He took it and offered it as a sacrifice to God in place of Isaac.

Together, he and Isaac went back down the mountain and returned home.

Isaac and Rebecca

Abraham was very old, and Sarah had already died, by the time Isaac had grown up. Abraham knew that he must find a wife for Isaac so that his family could increase and become the people of God.

He sent his most faithful servant, with a string of camels laden with gifts, to Mesopotamia to find a wife for Isaac from among his people there.

It was evening when the servant arrived: the time of day when the women came outside the gates of the city in order to fetch water from the well. Abraham's servant prayed, asking God to give him a sign to help him choose the right wife for Isaac. He would ask for a drink at the well. The young woman who offered to water his camels would be the one chosen by God.

Even before he had finished praying, a beautiful young woman came up to the well to fill her water jug. The servant asked her if she could spare him a drink.

"Drink, my lord," she said, and she held out her jug for him. "And when you have finished, I'll draw some water for your camels as well." The servant knew he had found the wife for Isaac.

The young woman's name was Rebecca. Her father gave his blessing to the marriage, and Rebecca was willing to return at once with Abraham's servant.

Early next morning they set out for Canaan. Isaac was praying out in the fields when he saw the camel train coming. He ran to meet them and took Rebecca by the hand. He loved her immediately. They married and lived together in great happiness.

Jacob's dream

Isaac and Rebecca had two sons. Esau, the eldest, became a hunter. He had the birthright to his father's inheritance. Jacob, the younger son, became a sheep farmer and was his mother's favourite. When Isaac was old and dying, Jacob tricked Esau out of his birthright with the help of his mother, Rebecca. But afterwards, Esau was so furious with his brother that Jacob had to flee for his life. He headed for Mesopotamia.

On the way, he stopped for the night in a lonely, rocky place, where he slept on the ground. That night Jacob had a strange dream. He saw a ladder stretching right up to heaven, and God's angels were going up and down it. Then he saw God himself standing beside him, saying, "I am the God of your grandfather Abraham, and your father Isaac. I shall be with you and bless you, and keep you safe. The land on which you are lying will be yours, and from you will come my chosen people. Your descendants will be as many as the dust on the ground."

When Jacob woke up he was amazed. "This is truly a holy place," he said. "It must be the very house of God and gate of heaven!"

Taking the stone on which he had rested his head during the night, Jacob set it up as a pillar, and poured oil over it. He named the place Bethel, which means "house of God". Then he made a solemn promise to God. "If the God of my fathers stays with me and keeps me safe, then he shall be my God, too."

Jacob went to live among his mother's people. He had two wives – Rachel and Leah – who gave him twelve sons, and he became very rich.

After many years he and his family returned to Canaan. The night before he crossed into the Promised Land, Jacob spent the night alone in prayer. A stranger appeared and wrestled with him all night.

"What is your name?" asked the stranger eventually. Jacob told him. "From now on your name shall be Israel." Jacob realised he had been wrestling with God.

The next day Jacob was finally reunited with his brother, Esau.

Joseph's wonderful coat

Of all his sons, Jacob loved Joseph, the second to youngest, the best.

When Joseph was seventeen, Jacob gave him a special coat to wear. It was woven with many colours and had long sleeves: the kind of coat that only a privileged, eldest son might own.

When Joseph's brothers saw how their father spoiled him, they were very jealous of Joseph and began to hate him.

Joseph used to have wonderful dreams, and he always knew what they meant. One day he told his brothers about his latest dream. "I dreamed that we were tying up sheaves of wheat that we had harvested. My sheaf stood up tall and straight, but all your sheaves bowed down to mine."

"Does this mean you think you are going to lord it over us?" cried his brothers, and they were so furious with him that they could not speak to him again.

Joseph had a second dream, similar to the first. This time he saw the sun, the moon and eleven stars all bowing down to him.

When he told his father about it, Jacob scolded him. "That's a fine dream to have!" he said. "Do you really think that one day your mother and I, and all your brothers, will bow down to you?"

Joseph's brothers, however, were so angry that they plotted how they might get rid of Joseph for good.

Joseph becomes a slave

One day Jacob sent Joseph to visit his brothers, who were far away up in the mountains with the sheep. While he was still a long way off, they saw him coming, wearing his colourful new coat.

"Here comes the dreamer," they said. "Let's kill him and throw his body into a pit. We can say he was caught by a wild animal."

"No," said Reuben, the eldest. "Let's just throw him into a pit and leave him to die." He didn't want to kill Joseph, but planned to come back later and rescue him.

When Joseph arrived, they grabbed him, took off his coat, and tossed him down into an empty well. Then they sat down to eat.

While they were having their meal, some merchants came along. Their camels were laden with spices and goods that the merchants hoped to sell in Egypt. One of Joseph's brothers had an idea.

"Let's sell Joseph to these merchants," he said, "then we won't have to kill him. After all, he is our brother." The others agreed. They hauled Joseph out of the well and sold him as a slave to the merchants for twenty pieces of silver.

Before returning home, the brothers dipped Joseph's coat in goat's blood. "Look what we've found, Father!" they cried, when they saw Jacob. "Isn't this the coat you gave Joseph?"

Jacob was horrified. "Yes, it's Joseph's coat! Some wild animal must have killed him!" And nothing anyone could say comforted him. He would grieve for Joseph for the rest of his life.

But Joseph was not dead – he was on his way to Egypt and God was looking after him.

Joseph in prison

Joseph was sold at the slave market to a man called Potiphar, who was an important officer in charge of the Royal Guard at the palace of the Pharaoh, or king.

Joseph became so good at his job that Potiphar put him in charge of his household. Then one day Potiphar's wife told her husband lies about Joseph, and Potiphar had him thrown into prison.

The keeper of the prison soon discovered that Joseph was special, too: he put him in charge of the other prisoners. Among them were the Pharaoh's butler and baker. One morning the two men told Joseph that they had each had a strange dream.

"My God has made me wise," said Joseph. "Describe your dreams and I will tell you what they mean."

"In my dream," said the butler, "I saw a grapevine with three bunches of grapes on it. I squeezed them into Pharaoh's wine cup and gave it to him to drink."

"The three bunches are three days," said Joseph. "In three days Pharaoh will forgive you and you will be serving him with wine again."

"In my dream," said the baker, "I was carrying three baskets of delicious pastries to Pharaoh. But some birds flew down and pecked at them."

"I'm afraid it means that in three days you will die," said Joseph.

It was Pharaoh's birthday in three days' time. Just as Joseph had said, Pharaoh took the butler back into his service, but he had the baker put to death.

The butler returned to his work and forgot all about Joseph.

Joseph the ruler of Egypt

Joseph remained in prison for another two years. Then one night Pharaoh himself had a strange dream. He dreamed he stood by a river. Seven fat cows came out of the water and ate the grass in the meadow. Then seven thin cows came out of the water. They ate up the seven fat cows, but stayed as thin as before!

None of Pharaoh's wise men and advisers could tell him what the dream meant. Suddenly, his butler remembered Joseph and told Pharaoh. Joseph was immediately fetched from prison.

"I hear you are wise and can interpret dreams," said Pharaoh.

"My God speaks through me," said Joseph, "and tells me what to say."

So Pharaoh described his dream. After thinking about it for a little while, Joseph told him what it meant.

"God has shown you the future, Pharaoh," he said. "There will be seven 'fat' years with plenty of food for everyone. Then there will be seven 'thin' years without rain, when everyone will be hungry. During the years of plenty, you should store all the grain from the harvest carefully so that there will be enough to last during the years of famine."

Pharaoh was very impressed with Joseph. "Your God has indeed filled you with wisdom," he said, and he gave Joseph the highest office in the land, second only to Pharaoh himself. Joseph was given rich clothes to wear and Pharaoh's own ring. He travelled through the country in his own chariot and everywhere he went, people bowed down before him.

Joseph sees his family again

For seven years, there was plenty of food. Joseph was put in charge of making sure that grain was stored carefully all over Egypt. Then came seven years without rain. Many regions went hungry, but not Egypt, and soon people started travelling to Egypt to buy food. Amongst them were Joseph's elder brothers.

Joseph knew them at once. But they did not recognise him.

Joseph accused them of being spies. They assured him they were not, but Joseph kept one brother as hostage and told the others to return home and fetch their youngest brother, to prove that their story was true. It was just a trick so that Joseph could see his brother Benjamin again.

The next time the brothers came to Egypt, they brought Benjamin with them. Joseph hid a silver cup inside the bag that Benjamin carried. Then, when the brothers tried to leave the palace, he had them arrested. Benjamin was ordered to remain in Egypt as a slave.

"That would break our father Jacob's heart," said the brothers. "Take one of us instead."

Joseph could not hide his secret from them any longer. Overcome with tears of joy, he told his brothers who he was, and begged them to hurry home to fetch their father, Jacob.

So it was that Jacob and his whole family came to live in Egypt, joyfully reunited with Joseph. The people of God lived in Egypt for many years, and Jacob's twelve sons eventually became the ancestors of the twelve tribes of Israel.

Baby Moses

The people of God – the Israelites – lived comfortably in Egypt for many years. Their numbers grew. Like Joseph, some of them became very rich and important.

All this changed when a new Pharaoh came to rule Egypt, who was afraid of them. He made all the Israelites slaves and put them to work making bricks and roads. He also ordered that any new boy child born to an Israelite woman should be killed. It seemed as if God had deserted his people.

One woman managed to save her son by putting him in a basket woven from bulrushes, which she hid among the reeds at the edge of the river. Her little daughter, Miriam, stayed nearby to watch.

Before long, Pharaoh's daughter came down to the river to bathe. She saw the basket in the reeds and sent her maid to fetch it. When the princess saw the crying infant, she realised he must be a slave baby and felt sorry for him.

Then Miriam came forward. "He's hungry," she said to the princess. "Would you

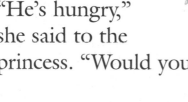

like me to fetch a slave woman to nurse him for you?"

The princess thought that was a good idea and so Miriam fetched her mother.

Pharaoh's daughter offered to pay the slave woman to nurse the child, and so the baby was brought up by his own mother.

When he had grown into a young boy, Pharaoh's daughter adopted him and called him Moses. He came to live in the palace with her and was taught to read and write like other royal children.

But Moses never forgot the God of his ancestors and the teachings of his real mother.

God calls Moses

Although he grew up in a palace, Moses knew that his people suffered greatly at the hands of the Egyptians and it made him very angry. One day he saw an Egyptian guard hitting a slave. Moses was so angry, he killed the guard and then had to flee for his own life.

He escaped into the desert of Midian, where he became a shepherd for a holy man called Jethro. Before long, he married Jethro's daughter.

One day, Moses was leading Jethro's sheep in search of water in the desert, when he came to the holy mountain of Sinai. There, Moses noticed a bush that seemed to be on fire, yet it did not burn away. He went to take a closer look, and suddenly the voice of God spoke: "Moses, do not come any nearer. Take off your sandals, for this is holy ground. I am the God of your ancestors, the God of Abraham, the God of Isaac and the God of Jacob."

Moses knelt and covered his face, he was so afraid.

"I have seen the suffering of my people and heard their prayers for help," God said,

"and I want you to go back to Egypt to set them free. Tell them I sent you."

"But what if they won't listen to me?" asked Moses. "What if they don't believe you have sent me?"

"Throw your staff on the ground," said God. Moses did as God asked. Immediately the staff turned into a snake and Moses leaped back in fear. "Pick it up by the tail," said God. Moses did so and it turned back into a staff. "With this," said God, "you will convince them that the Lord God of their fathers has really sent you."

Moses the leader

God gave Moses the courage to go back to Egypt and tell Pharaoh to release the Israelites. Pharaoh refused and instead made the slaves work harder than ever. The Israelites became angry with Moses for making the situation worse.

When Pharaoh refused to free the slaves, Moses warned him that Egypt would suffer nine plagues, or disasters.

First the river turned into blood, killing all the fish and making the water smell terrible. Then the whole of Egypt was plagued by swarms of frogs.

Pharaoh remained stubborn.

Next came gnats, then flies, then disease, which killed all the livestock, and boils which caused misery for everyone. The seventh plague was hailstorms that flattened the crops, followed by locusts which turned the sky black and ate every green leaf that remained.

Still Pharaoh remained stubborn and refused to free the Israelites from slavery.

Finally darkness covered the land for three days. Everyone knew these were signs from God, but Pharaoh refused to do as Moses asked.

Finally, Moses promised a plague more terrible than all the others. At midnight, all the first-born children and animals in the land would die – including Pharaoh's own son. Only the children of God's chosen people would be spared.

The first Passover

God told Moses exactly what the Israelites must do to ensure that the angel of death did not visit them that night. Each household had to kill a lamb and roast it with herbs. Everyone should eat quickly, standing up, dressed and ready to escape into the desert. They should eat the meat with unleavened bread (that is, made without yeast) and smear some of the blood from the lamb on the doorposts of their homes. The angel would pass over all those houses marked in this way.

The Israelites were to keep this day, which would be known as the Passover, a holy feast in honour of the Lord, every year, for ever more.

The Israelites did as Moses had told them.

At midnight, the angel of the Lord passed over the land and took the lives of all the firstborn in each household. Not one house was spared. But the angel passed by the Israelite houses marked with blood, just as the Lord had promised.

Pharaoh, overcome with grief at the death of his son – the heir to the throne of Egypt – summoned Moses to him in the middle of the night and ordered him to take the slaves, together with all their sheep and cattle, and leave Egypt as soon as they could.

And so, after four hundred and thirty years of slavery, the six hundred thousand Hebrews took all their belongings and walked out of Egypt and into the desert, with Moses leading them and the Lord guiding his people with a pillar of cloud.

Escape from Pharaoh

God led his chosen people through the desert towards the Red Sea. By day they followed the pillar of cloud, and at night they followed a pillar of fire, so they were able to travel by night and day and not lose their way.

Meanwhile, Pharaoh changed his mind. "What have I done allowing the Hebrews to leave my service?" he asked. Furious, he sent out his army to recapture the slaves and bring them back for punishment.

When they saw the dust cloud caused by the galloping horses and chariots behind them, and the Red Sea in front of them, the Israelites were terrified. They accused Moses of leading them to their deaths.

"Do not be afraid!" said Moses. "The Lord God will keep us safe!"

Moses stretched out his hand over the sea. A fierce wind arose and drove back the sea to right and left, leaving a channel of dry land. The people hurried across.

Pharaoh's army saw the channel through the Red Sea and galloped after them. Suddenly, the wind dropped and the waters rolled back, trapping the Egyptians in the mud and waves. No one escaped.

That day, the people sang songs and danced in honour of the Lord God:

Sing of the Lord: he has covered himself in glory.
Horse and rider he has thrown into the sea!

Moses the law-giver

Moses led the people to the mountain of Sinai, where God had first spoken to him. Here, God gave Moses two stone slabs on which were the laws by which his chosen people were to live their lives.

On the first stone were the laws concerning their duty to God. They must not worship other gods. They must not worship idols of wood or stone. They must keep God's name holy. They must keep God's day – the Sabbath – holy. And they must honour their parents.

The second tablet contained the laws concerning their duty to each other. They must not kill. They must not be unfaithful to their wife or husband. They must not steal anything. They must not tell lies. They must not be envious of another person.

These were the Ten Commandments which God gave to his chosen people through Moses. On Sinai, God made a solemn agreement – a covenant – with his people: they were to promise to live by these commandments, and God in turn would promise to be their God, and they his chosen people for all time.

Joshua the leader

Moses led the people of God to Canaan, the land God had promised to Abraham. It was a country full of good things, but the cities were well-defended with high walls. Then Moses knew he had to hand over the task of taking the people to the Promised Land to another leader. God chose Joshua to replace Moses: "Be strong and brave, Joshua, for I will always be with you."

Then Moses blessed the people one last time and climbed up to the summit of Mount Pisgah. Here, within sight of the Promised Land, Moses died.

Joshua led the chosen people in a procession across

the River Jordan and on to the city of Jericho. With
trumpets sounding, the Ark of the Covenant was carried
round the city for six days. On the seventh day, the
people went round the city seven times. Then the priests
sounded the trumpets, the people shouted, and the walls
collapsed, so Joshua and his army could take the city.

At last the Israelites could live in Canaan in peace.

Joshua divided the land fairly amongst the twelve
tribes, named after Jacob's (Israel's) sons. Only the tribe
of Levi did not ask for a share of land: it was their
special calling to provide priests to serve God.

The call of Gideon

As time passed, the chosen people forgot the God of their ancestors and started worshipping other gods. So God sent them a new enemy, the Midianites, fierce tribesmen who raided farms, stealing crops and animals. After seven years of this, the Israelites once more turned to God and asked him for help.

God called on Gideon, a humble farmer's son. He promised to help Gideon destroy the Midianites with a very small army, but first of all, he told Gideon to smash all the altars to the other gods.

Gideon's army of volunteers seemed far too small.
He only had three hundred men. Nevertheless, God
promised him victory.

Gideon attacked the Midianite camp at night. He
gave each of his men a trumpet and a lighted torch
hidden in a jug. As soon as he gave the signal, the men
blew their trumpets, broke the jugs and held their lamps
up high as they charged. All the noise and lights made
the Midianites think they were being attacked by a huge
army. They fled in terror.

So God kept his promise. The Midianites never
troubled his people again.

The story of Ruth

There was a widow living in Moab, called Naomi. She had lived there with her husband and two sons who had both married Moabite women. Now her husband and sons were dead, Naomi longed to return to her own country.

Her daughter-in-law, Ruth, decided to go with her. "I want your home to be my home," said Ruth, "and your God to be my God."

The two women came to Bethlehem, where they made their home near land owned by Boaz, a relative of Naomi's husband.

Each day Ruth went out into the fields and picked up the stalks of corn left behind after the harvest, to feed herself and Naomi. One day Boaz himself noticed her.

"Who is this young woman?" he asked his servant. "Does she belong to anyone?"

"She is the Moabite woman who came back with Naomi after her husband died." The servant told Boaz just how hard Ruth worked.

Boaz was impressed with Ruth. He arranged for his reapers to leave extra corn in Ruth's path, and told her to stay in his own fields, where she would be safe.

Ruth fell on her knees and thanked him. "What have I done to deserve your kindness?" she asked him.

"I have heard how kind you have been to your mother-in-law," said Boaz. "May the Lord God reward you."

In time, Boaz took Ruth to be his wife and the Lord blessed her with a son whom they called Obed.

Obed would become the father of Jesse – the father of David.

The call of Samuel

One day a woman brought her son Samuel to the temple at Shiloh, where the Ark of the Covenant was kept, and left him with Eli, the priest in charge. She had promised God that if he gave her a son, she would give him to the temple, to serve God.

One night, when Samuel lay sleeping, he was woken by a voice calling: "Samuel! Samuel!" He thought it was Eli calling, so he ran to see what Eli wanted.

"I did not call you, my son. Go back to bed," said Eli. But Samuel heard the voice again, and again he ran to Eli. The third time it happened Eli realised that it was God calling the boy.

"If you hear the voice again," he told Samuel, "say 'Speak, Lord. Your servant is listening.'"

Samuel did just as Eli had told him. From that moment, God spoke to Samuel. And as he grew up, all God's people knew that he was God's prophet – his special messenger – and honoured him.

Samuel chooses a king

The people of God had a very strong enemy at this time: the Philistines. They attacked the Israelites and tried to take over the Promised Land. Some of the elders went to Samuel and asked him to choose a king to lead them into battle. Samuel asked God for advice.

"Do as they ask," said the Lord God. "It is me they have rejected, not you. They no longer want me to lead them. But you must tell them exactly what it means to have a king."

Samuel went back to the elders and explained to them that a king would take their sons and make them serve as soldiers in his army. He would take their daughters to work for him, the best of their land and a tenth of their flocks. But the people still insisted on having a king so they could be like other nations.

So Samuel chose a handsome young man called Saul. He consecrated Saul to the service of God by anointing him with holy oil, and proclaimed him king.

In a very short time, Saul raised an army and fought well against the Philistines. But he became proud and hard. He broke important religious laws and refused to obey Samuel.

"Since you have rejected God," said Samuel, "so God has rejected you as king."

Samuel never saw Saul again. Instead, he went under God's guidance to find a new king for the chosen people.

Samuel chooses David

S amuel was upset by Saul's disobedience and often, when he thought about Saul, his eyes would fill with tears. When God saw Samuel weeping for Saul, he asked, "How long will you mourn for Saul? You know I have rejected him and he will not be king."

Then God told Samuel to fill his horn with oil and sent him to the town of Bethlehem. A farmer named Jesse lived there, and God had chosen one of Jesse's sons to be the next king.

At first, Samuel was afraid to go. "If Saul hears of this, he will kill me," he said.

Samuel arrived in Bethlehem and ordered a feast in honour of the Lord God. It was an exciting occasion for the town, and everyone attended including Jesse and all his family.

One by one, Jesse introduced each of his seven sons to Samuel. They were all tall, handsome young men, and as he met each one Samuel thought, "Surely this young man must be God's choice!"

But every time a voice inside Samuel's head said, "No, not this one." It was very puzzling.

"Are these all your sons?" he asked Jesse.

"Except for David, my youngest," said Jesse. "He's looking after the sheep."

Samuel said they couldn't begin the feast until David arrived. They sent for the young man, and he arrived looking bright, handsome and fit.

"This is the one I have chosen," said God to Samuel. "Anoint him king!"

Samuel anointed David with holy oil in front of his brothers. He would be king of Israel one day, but in the meantime he was to return to his sheep. From that moment, the spirit of the Lord was close to David in a special way.

David and his harp

D avid loved to play the harp and sing while he spent
lonely days and nights watching over his sheep,
and he became famous for his songs.

King Saul at this time was very ill. He suffered from
fits of madness and depression which only music could
soothe. His servants told him he should send for a
skilled musician: someone who could play for him
whenever he had one of these attacks of illness, and

so bring him relief. "Find me such a man!" said Saul.

One of the king's soldiers told them about Jesse's son, David. He was not only a good musician, but he had courage and was a man of God.

Messengers were sent to Jesse from the king, asking that David should come and play for the king.

And so whenever King Saul needed him, David left his flocks to come and play sweet, gentle music to soothe the king's madness. King Saul came to love this young man from Bethlehem who was able to bring peace and calm to his troubled mind.

David and Goliath

Three of David's brothers were soldiers in King Saul's army. One morning, Jesse sent David out to them with supplies of food. He reached his brothers in time to see a giant of a man – over three metres tall – step from the ranks of the Philistine army. Goliath challenged the Israelites to send out a champion to fight him in single combat and finish the war quickly.

The soldiers of King Saul were terrified of him.

"I'll go and fight him!" said David. But King Saul would not allow it, saying David was only a boy.

David told Saul about the times he had killed a lion and a bear while guarding his sheep. God had helped him then, and he would help him now. Reluctantly, Saul allowed him to take up Goliath's challenge.

David refused to wear armour or carry a sword. Instead, he went down to the river and picked out five smooth stones, which he put in his shepherd's pouch. With his sling in his hand, he went to face Goliath.

Goliath roared with laughter and scorned such a small champion. David put a stone in his sling. He whirled the sling around his head and the stone struck Goliath on the forehead, knocking him out. David then took Goliath's own sword and cut off the giant's head.

When the Philistines saw their champion was dead, they fled.

David in hiding

David became a fine soldier and King Saul made him commander of his army. He was handsome, brave and popular and the people sang his praises instead of praising Saul. He was also a close friend of the king's son, Jonathan. Saul saw all this and grew mad with jealousy.

One day the king suddenly threw his spear at David. It missed its target, but David had to flee for his life. From then on, David had to hide from the king and his men, who searched everywhere for David, to kill him.

One night, Saul and his guard came into the cave where David was hiding, to rest. David would not harm Saul, but while they slept, he cut off a piece of Saul's robe. When dawn came, David followed Saul out of the cave and showed him the piece of cloth.

"My lord king," he said, "I could have killed you, but I am your loyal servant. Why do you want to kill me?" Saul was overcome with grief, but not for long.

Soon after, Saul went to war with the Philistines again. This time he was wounded and his three sons were slain. When he saw that the Philistines had won the battle and his sons were dead, Saul killed himself.

When David heard of their deaths, he was very sad.

David the king

Now that Saul was dead, David could return to his own land. His own tribe of Judah made him their king, as Samuel had anointed him when he was a boy.

Saul's remaining sons ruled in the north. But in time they died too, and so David became king over all the tribes of Israel. When the Philistines heard the news, they marched against him, but David defeated them in battle. Never again did they attack the people of God.

David conquered other lands, too, and made a great kingdom. He needed a capital city. He chose a strong fortress called Jerusalem, set high on a hill in the middle of the kingdom. But he had to take it from the Jebusites who lived there, and refused to let him enter the gates.

David sent some men secretly into the tunnel that ran under the wall of the city, carrying the water supply. They came up inside the city and opened the gates so David and his army could take the Jebusites by surprise.

Jerusalem became David's city.

Jerusalem, city of God

King David had captured the fortress of Jerusalem and made it the capital city of his kingdom. This is where he had his court, and where he ruled over Israel.

But David wanted Jerusalem to be God's city, too, where God might live among his chosen people. So he decided that the sacred Ark of the Covenant, that held the sacred stone tablets on which were written the commandments of God, should be brought to Jerusalem. While the Ark was with them, the people knew that God was with them, too.

David sent for the Ark and it was brought to the city in a great procession of rejoicing people. Musicians played and David was so happy that he threw off his royal robes and joined in the dancing with everyone else. He just wanted to give praise and glory to God.

The Ark was carried to a special tent, where it would remain until a temple could be built for it.

So the city of Jerusalem became the city of God.

David and Absalom

King David had many sons and he loved them all dearly. But as David grew old, they started quarrelling with each other. Only one of them could be king of Israel when their father died. David knew about the squabbles but he did nothing to stop them.

One day, David's eldest son, Amnon, was murdered by his half-brother, Absalom. Absalom then went into hiding and raised an army against David, so he could make himself king. When David heard of this, the first thing he did was to leave Jerusalem so that the city would not be attacked. Then he told his soldiers that he did not want any harm to come to his son Absalom.

During the battle between the two armies, Absalom rode his mule under an oak tree and his long hair caught in its branches. His mule ran off, leaving Absalom hanging and unable to free himself. David's soldiers found Absalom and killed him.

David waited impatiently for news of the battle, but his men were afraid to tell him. When at last he heard that they had won, but that Absalom had been killed, David was overcome with grief. "Oh, Absalom, my son, my son," he wept. "I wish I had died instead of you!"

There was no rejoicing over the victory that day. Instead, David's troops returned from the battlefield quietly and stealthily, as if they were ashamed.

Later, another of David's sons tried to become king, but David chose his son Solomon to be king after him.

Solomon's dream

Solomon was anointed king just before David died. Although David had given him a great deal of advice, once his father was dead Solomon realised just how difficult it would be to rule a kingdom by himself.

Like David, Solomon had a great love for God, so he went to the holy place at Gibeon where he offered sacrifices to God and prayed for guidance.

During the night, God appeared to him in a dream.

"Ask me for what you want most, and I will give it to you," he said.

Solomon replied, "You have chosen me to be king, Lord, after my father David. You showed him great mercy when he followed your ways. Now you have brought me to the throne. But I am young and inexperienced, and I am king over a great nation. Give me, therefore, a wise heart so that I can be a good ruler for your people."

God was very pleased with Solomon's answer. "You could have asked for a long life, or riches, or success over your enemies, but instead you have asked for wisdom. I will do as you ask. I am therefore giving you a wise and understanding heart so that you will be a good king. You will be unique. There is no one to compare with you before, nor will there be anyone after your death. And because you asked for wisdom, I will also give you those things you didn't ask for: a long life, riches, and victory over your enemies. Just keep my commandments, like your father, and I will give you all these things."

Solomon became a wise king. Over three thousand of his clever sayings – called proverbs – were written into books by the skilled writers of his court, and, in addition, Solomon wrote many songs and poems. He became famous among his people for his wisdom and knowledge, especially of the natural world, and his fame spread to other lands. Many people came from around the world to ask his advice and bring him gifts.

Solomon the wise

One day two women came to Solomon's court with a baby boy.

One of them said, "My lord, this woman and I live in the same house. I gave birth to a baby boy. There was no one else in the house at the time. Then, this woman's baby died one night, so she came to my room, took my baby while I was asleep and put her dead baby in its place. When I woke to feed the baby I knew at once that it wasn't my child."

"No! That's not right!" said the other woman. "This baby is mine. The dead child was hers!"

Solomon turned to his officer. "Fetch me a sword," he said. When the sword was brought, he said, "Now, cut the child in half, and give half to each woman."

The woman who was the child's real mother threw herself at the king's feet. "Please, my lord," she begged him, "give the child to her. Do not think of killing him."

But the other woman said, "The baby won't belong to either of us. Cut him up."

Solomon made his decision. "Give the child to the first woman. Do not kill him. She is his real mother."

The whole of Israel came to hear of this story, and everyone recognised that God had indeed blessed Solomon with great wisdom.

The temple of Solomon

David had brought the sacred Ark of the Covenant to Jerusalem. Now his son Solomon started work on a beautiful temple, four years after he became king.

Builders came from Phoenicia. Cedar, cypress and juniper wood were brought by sea. Blocks of special stone were cut from the mountains. Gold and silver came from other lands. Thousands upon thousands of workers were employed.

The huge doors were made of bronze. Walls were made of cedar wood, carved with flowers and trees. Altars were made of cedar wood and covered in gold.

The inner temple, the holy of holies where the Ark of the Covenant was to be kept, was entirely covered in gold.

It took seven years for the temple of Jerusalem to be finished. At last, in solemn procession, the priests of Levi carried the sacred chest from the tent to the holy of holies. As they left, a cloud filled the temple, so thick that the priests were unable to continue the service. It was the glory of the Lord God.

King Solomon turned to face the people. In the hush, he told them that God had come to dwell among them in the temple. Then he led them in a great prayer that God would always bless his house and his people who worshipped him there.

God appeared to Solomon a second time. "I grant your prayer," he said, "and I consecrate this temple you

have built. My eyes and my heart shall always be here. If you walk with me and keep my commandments, I shall make your royal throne secure over Israel, just as I promised David your father. But if you turn away from me, and worship other gods, then I will cut Israel off from the land I have given them, and leave the temple for ever."

Solomon in all his glory

Solomon became rich as well as wise, as God had promised. He had inherited a huge kingdom from his father, David, and had married an Egyptian princess. All the lands belonging to his kingdom had to pay taxes to him, and he became famous for his wealth. For the whole of Solomon's reign, there was peace in the Promised Land.

Solomon had a huge army with one thousand, four hundred chariots and twelve thousand horses. The ships of his navy sailed down the Red Sea to trade with other countries, bringing back gold, silver, exotic birds, ivory and spices. Caravans of camels travelled over the desert to bring precious goods to the royal court.

Solomon built a magnificent palace for himself at Jerusalem that took thirteen years to complete. He was helped by Hiram, king of Tyre, an old friend of his father. One day the Queen of Sheba came to visit Solomon, to ask his advice and see for herself whether he was as rich as she had heard. She brought him a great many costly gifts from Arabia: spices, gold and precious stones.

The queen was amazed. "All that I heard is true," she said. "Your wisdom and glory are even greater than I expected. Happy are your people. Blessed be your God, and great is his love that he should have made you so wise, glorious and great."

Solomon turns away from God

King Solomon may have been very rich, but he still managed to spend more than he could afford. Whenever he went into debt, he made the people pay heavy taxes. When he needed workmen for his building projects, he sent out officials to force men to come and work for him as slaves. He paid them no wages.

Solomon had a great many wives from many different countries and they each had their own religious beliefs. Instead of teaching them about the Lord God, Solomon built temples for their own gods and as he grew older, he began to worship these foreign gods as well.

This made God very sad. He had hoped that Solomon, like David, would remain faithful to him. God finally said to Solomon, "Since you have broken your promises, I am going to take your kingdom away from you and give it to one of your servants. For your father David's sake this will not happen in your own lifetime, but in that of your son's. And for the sake of Jerusalem, I will leave you one tribe."

Solomon ruled over Israel in Jerusalem for forty years. When he died, his son Rehoboam became king. But the northern tribes rebelled against Rehoboam and the kingdom was divided into two: Israel in the north and Judah in the south.

Elijah in the desert

Ahab became king of Israel. His wife, Jezebel, brought from her own country hundreds of priests of Baal, and set about executing all the prophets of the Lord God she could find.

As a result of their wickedness, God sent his prophet, Elijah, to warn King Ahab that there would be a drought in Israel lasting many years.

After delivering his message, Elijah had to hide in the desert, to escape from Jezebel. Each day ravens brought him bread and meat to eat and he drank from a brook.

When the brook dried up, God sent Elijah to the city of Sidon.

At the city gates, Elijah met a widow gathering sticks. He asked her for a drink of water and some food.

"I have no bread," said the woman, "but only a handful of flour in a jar and a little oil in a jug. I shall make my son and myself a last meal, and then we will die."

"Don't be afraid," said Elijah. "Cook your meal, but bring some for me as well, and you will find that the jar of flour will never be used up, or the jug of oil emptied, until this drought comes to an end."

There was not only enough food for them all, but the flour and oil never ran out, just as Elijah had promised.

Then the widow's son became very ill and died. "Why have you allowed my son to be taken from me?" she demanded of Elijah. Elijah took the boy and prayed over him, and after a while he came back to life.

Overjoyed, the widow said, "Now I know that you are a man of God and the word of God that you speak is truth."

Elijah and the prophets of Baal

The drought in Israel lasted three years. Then Elijah returned to King Ahab and challenged him to prove that Baal was a greater god than the Lord God of Israel.

"Tell all the people of Israel, and the four hundred and fifty prophets of Baal, to meet me on Mount Carmel," he said to Ahab.

There, he ordered them to prepare an altar and sacrifice to Baal while he built an altar to God. But they were not to set fire to it yet.

"Let he who is the true God set fire to the wood," said Elijah.

When their altar was complete, the prophets of Baal prayed to their god to bring fire for them. For hours they cried out to Baal and danced round and round their altar. But no voice answered them, and no fire lit their wood. Elijah laughed at them. "Cry louder," he said. "Perhaps your god has gone out. Or maybe he is asleep. Try shouting louder to wake him up."

Elijah built his own altar out of twelve stones – one for each tribe of Israel – covered it with wood and dug a deep trench round it. He prepared his sacrifice and put it on the altar. Then he told the people to pour water over the altar until it was all completely soaked and water filled the trench.

"God of Abraham, Isaac and Jacob," he prayed, "send fire, so that your people will know that you are God in Israel and that I am your servant." Instantly, the

soaking wood burst into flames. The wood, stones and
the offering on the altar – even the water in the trench
around it – were completely burned up by the fire.

When the people saw this, they fell down and
worshipped God.

And rain came again to Israel: the drought was over.

Elijah the champion of God

King Ahab had built a beautiful palace in the town of Jezreel. It had a lovely garden, but there was nowhere to grow vegetables. Just next door to the garden, however, there was a vineyard owned by a poor man called Naboth.

The king said to Naboth, "I'd like to buy your vineyard for my vegetable garden. Name your price: I'll pay you well for it."

But Naboth shook his head. "The vineyard was left to me by my father. I cannot sell it," he said. It was unthinkable for a man to sell his inheritance.

Ahab was very angry and disappointed.

When Jezebel heard what had happened, she laughed scornfully.

"You're supposed to be the king!" she said. "Never mind. I'll get you Naboth's vineyard!"

Jezebel sent a letter to the chief councillors of Jezreel, ordering them to put Naboth on trial for crimes against God. She arranged for two men to give false evidence to show Naboth was guilty. The councillors were scared of Jezebel, so they did as she had commanded. Naboth was found guilty and put to death.

"Naboth is dead!" Jezebel told Ahab, triumphantly. "The vineyard is yours."

Ahab ran down eagerly to take possession of the vineyard, but when he got there he found Elijah the prophet waiting for him.

"God has sent me," said Elijah. "You and your queen have done a great evil, and God will bring terrible punishment on you and your family!"

Then Ahab was filled with guilt and sorrow for all the things he had done wrong. He took off his royal robes and wore rough sackcloth instead. When he walked, it was slowly and gloomily to show everyone how sorry he was for his wickedness.

God was pleased with Ahab's change of heart. He decided not to punish Ahab in his own lifetime, but made sure that his family were no longer kings of Israel.

Elisha and the lady from Shunem

When Elijah's days were over, God passed on his power to Elisha. Everyone loved Elisha. He travelled the country, teaching people and helping them.

In a town called Shunem, a rich farmer's wife had suggested to her husband that they built Elisha a little room on the flat roof of their house. Elisha was delighted. "I wish I knew how to thank her," he said to his servant. "But she is rich and doesn't need anything."

The servant told him, "She would love to have a son."

"By this time next year," Elisha said to the lady, "you will hold a son in your arms."

It happened just as Elisha promised. But one day, the little boy became very ill and died in his mother's arms. She laid his body on Elisha's bed in the little room. Then she ran to find Elisha.

Elisha returned with her, shut the door to his room, and prayed. He lay over the child's body to warm it, breathing air into his mouth. Suddenly, the boy sneezed.

"Your son is alive," Elisha called to the mother.

Elisha and the Syrian general

At that time, Israel was at war with Syria. The Syrian army, led by a great general called Naaman, made raids over the border of Israel, taking whatever they could find, including slaves. Among them was a young girl, who became the servant of General Naaman's wife.

Now General Naaman developed a terrible skin disease called leprosy. No one knew how to cure it. He would have to give up everything and live alone till he died. The Syrian girl often found her mistress weeping bitterly in her room. She felt so sorry for her.

"If only my master could go to my homeland," the girl told her mistress, "there is a holy man there called Elisha. He could heal him."

The general's wife told her husband what her servant had said, and Naaman told the king of Syria.

"Go to the king of Israel and ask him for a cure," said the king. "I will give you a letter for him, as well as gold and gifts."

But the king of Israel tore his robe and said, "Who does he think I am? I can't cure him! It's just an excuse to start another war!"

Elisha heard what had happened. "Send the general to me," he said to the king. "I will show him that there is a prophet of God in Israel."

When Naaman arrived at Elisha's house, a messenger told him to go and bathe seven times in the River Jordan, and he would be cured.

Naaman was furious. "I was sure Elisha would come out to me, call on his God and pray over me. What's so special about the River Jordan? Why couldn't I have bathed in any of the rivers in Damascus?"

"Master," said his servant. "If the prophet had asked you to do something difficult, you'd have done it, wouldn't you? All the more reason, then, to do the simple thing he has asked."

So Naaman did as he was told. When he had finished bathing, his leprosy had disappeared.

"Now I know," said Naaman, "that there is no God in all the earth except in Israel."

Isaiah saves Jerusalem

The people of Judah and Israel fell further and further away from God's laws, and God withdrew his help. After an invading army from Assyria had conquered the northern kingdom, the king of Judah, Hezekiah, who loved and served God, made a treaty with the Assyrians, so that they would not invade the south.

King Hezekiah was forced to strip the great temple of Jerusalem of some of its treasures in order to pay the Assyrians' demands. But instead of leaving, they surrounded the city and told the people to surrender.

Hezekiah asked Isaiah, a very holy man, for advice.

"The Assyrians will not conquer Jerusalem," said Isaiah. "This is God's promise."

Then the king of Assyria reminded Hezekiah of all the kingdoms they had destroyed. God did not help them: he would not help Judah either. Hezekiah went to the temple and prayed, asking God to save Jerusalem.

A messenger came from Isaiah, saying: "God has heard you. He will not allow Jerusalem to be taken."

That night, many thousands of Assyrian soldiers died from a terrible illness. The rest fled back to their own country, leaving Jerusalem safe.

Isaiah's warning

Hezekiah became very ill. Everyone expected him to die, but he prayed earnestly to God, and with Isaiah's help, he recovered.

Not long afterwards, an ambassador came to see him from Babylon, bringing presents from the Babylonian king, who had heard of Hezekiah's illness. Hezekiah was delighted with the visit, and eagerly showed the ambassador all over the palace, including the treasury, the armoury and the storehouses.

Isaiah came to the palace afterwards. "Where has this ambassador come from?" he asked Hezekiah. "What have you shown him?"

Hezekiah explained that the ambassador came from the distant country of Babylon, and that he had shown him everything.

"Listen, Hezekiah," said Isaiah. "The day will come when everything in your palace will be carried off to Babylon. Nothing will be left. Even your sons will be taken to the palace there."

But Hezekiah was not worried. As long as he enjoyed peace in his own lifetime, he was not concerned with what might follow.

Josiah and the discovery in the temple

Josiah was only eight when he became king of Judah. He loved God dearly and was anxious to bring the chosen people back to the God of his ancestor, David. The last king had made the people worship Baal, and had allowed the temple at Jerusalem to fall into ruins.

In his eighteenth year, Josiah undertook to repair the temple. One morning the king's secretary came to Josiah with an old scroll of parchment. "This was found in the rubbish in the temple," he said. It was a long-lost book of the Law. When Josiah heard what was written on the

scroll, he became very upset. He understood just how far his people had fallen from the laws of God.

Josiah called everyone together at the temple of Jerusalem, and read out to them the commandments written on the scroll. Together they all made a solemn promise to God to live by his laws: to love and worship him alone and follow the teachings that were written.

Then Josiah went through the land, tearing down and burning every last trace of Baal worship: every temple, altar and shrine.

Exiles in Babylon

After Josiah had died, the people of God once again forgot their promises to keep his law and they ignored the warnings of his prophet, Jeremiah. Jerusalem was conquered by the invading armies of Babylon, ruled by King Nebuchadnezzar. They stole the temple treasures, knocked down the walls and burned the entire city to the ground. The people of Judah – among them a young boy called Daniel – were marched into Babylon. Only the old and sick were left behind.

Just as Isaiah had foretold, God's chosen people had lost their land, their holy city and their temple. Even their king was a prisoner. Despite the beauty of the city of Babylon, they were in a strange land and homesick. They made sad songs telling of their unhappiness:

> *We sat down by the waters of Babylon, and we wept when we remembered Jerusalem. We hung our harps on the willow trees.*

But they still had hope. God was with them, even in exile, and their king still lived. Through his prophets, Jeremiah and Ezekiel, God instructed his people to settle in Babylon and live according to his commandments. One day he would restore their fortunes and return them to the land of their fathers.

"The days are coming," said the Lord, "when I shall make a new covenant with my people. I shall forgive them and forget the things they have done wrong."

Nehemiah rebuilds Jerusalem

When he conquered Babylon, the Persian king decided to let the Jewish people return to their homeland. He also gave back the treasures stolen from the temple of Jerusalem. But war prevented work to rebuild the city.

Nehemiah, a high official in the court of the Persian king, was one of the Jewish people who still lived in Bablyon. He had heard that the walls of the city of his ancestor, David, were still in ruins and the city gates had been burned to ashes, and it made him very sad. He wanted to go there himself and rebuild the walls.

The king granted him permission to go, and gave him letters to the governors of Jerusalem, ordering them to help Nehemiah. But before he introduced himself to the officials, Nehemiah secretly assessed the work that needed to be done.

Then he called the leaders of the people together. He showed them the royal letters. "God has sent me to rebuild the city walls," he told them. "I want each family to build one part. Here are your orders."

It seemed an impossible task, but Nehemiah drove the people on until the work was finished. Then at last the great day arrived when the new buildings could be dedicated to God. Celebrations went on for seven days and marked a new beginning for the people of God.

Stories of the Prophets

Throughout history, God chose men and women to speak for him and pass on his messages to the people about things that were going to happen. These were the "prophets". They were not particularly clever, rich or gifted: very often they did not want to be God's messengers at all, because they knew that they would be unpopular. But God always gave them the strength and gifts they needed to do his work.

Jeremiah

Jeremiah was a quiet, gentle young man. He came from a priestly family that lived near Jerusalem. When God called him to be a prophet, Jeremiah knew immediately how difficult this task would be for him.

"Ah, Lord," he said, "I really don't know how to speak: I am only a child!"

God, however, told him not to be afraid. He touched Jeremiah's mouth and said, "There! I have put my words into your mouth. Today I have put you in charge over nations and kingdoms, to uproot and knock down, to destroy and overthrow, to build and to plant."

He sent Jeremiah to a potter's house.
There he saw the potter making a clay pot,
but the pot lost its shape and so the
potter wet the clay, made it into a ball
once more and started again.
This time the pot was perfect.

God told Jeremiah that the people were like clay in
his hands. If they continued to live wickedly he would
destroy them. But if they kept his commandments and
were sorry for what they had done wrong, he would
make them good and strong.

Jeremiah went to the priests and wise men of Israel
and held up a pottery jar for them to see. Then he
smashed it to the ground, breaking it into small pieces.
"This is what will happen to the people of Judah," he
said, "if they do not listen to the word of the Lord!"

Jeremiah in prison

Jeremiah's warnings were ignored, and before long, as he had promised, Jerusalem was captured by the army of Babylon. The people rebelled, but Jeremiah warned them to leave the city: disaster was coming!

The city leaders hated the prophet. He was arrested and thrown into a dark, underground prison. Then they went to the king and demanded that Jeremiah should be put to death. "He's a traitor!" they said.

"Do what you want with him," said the cowardly king.

They were afraid to kill a man of God. Instead, they lowered Jeremiah into a deep well. He sank into the soft mud at the bottom and was left to die.

One of the royal servants heard what had happened and told the king. "My lord king," he said, "these men have done a wicked thing. Jeremiah will starve." The king then gave the servant permission to rescue Jeremiah.

Taking thirty men to help him, he dropped some rags down to Jeremiah to put under his arms, and ropes to tie over them. Then they pulled Jeremiah out of the well.

Jeremiah was saved from death, but his words of warning from God were still ignored.

Daniel in the lions' den

Daniel was a boy when the people of God were taken captive into Babylon. He grew up to be a good, wise young man, faithful to God, with a gift of being able to understand the meaning of dreams. It was this gift which brought him favour and rich rewards from the king, who made him ruler of the kingdom.

The other princes and nobles of Babylon were jealous of Daniel. They tricked the king into signing a new law that said no one could pray to any god except the king. Anyone caught disobeying this law would be thrown into the den of lions.

Three times a day, Daniel opened his window that faced Jerusalem, went down on his knees and prayed to the Lord God. It was easy for the officials to arrest him.

"We caught him praying to his God," they told the king. And although the king was deeply distressed, he had no choice but to give the order for Daniel to die.

So Daniel was thrown into the den of lions.

That night, the king was unable to eat or sleep. As soon as it was light, he hurried to the lions' den. "Daniel!" he cried. "Has your God been able to save you from the lions?"

"May your majesty live for ever!" said Daniel, cheerfully. "My God sent his angel to seal the lions' jaws. They did me no harm."

The king ordered Daniel to be released, and sent a message all over his kingdom about the goodness of the God of Daniel:

"He is the living God. His kingdom will last for ever. He saves, sets free and works signs and wonders in the heavens and on the earth."

Hosea

Hosea came from the northern kingdom of Israel. He married a woman called Gomer, and they had three children. At first they were very happy together. Hosea loved his quiet family life but Gomer grew tired of it. One day she put on her best clothes and her jewellery, and left to have a good time in the city.

Hosea was heartbroken. He loved Gomer very much. He went from town to town until he found Gomer and brought her back home. He pleaded with her to be faithful to him and their children, but again and again Gomer left him, breaking Hosea's heart.

Hosea had to bring up his children by himself, but even they left him as soon as they could.

Hosea's unhappy marriage taught him a great deal about God and his love for his people. Israel, the bride of God, had become unfaithful to him and turned away from his law again and again. God would punish Israel, but only to bring her back into his loving arms.

Amos the shepherd

Amos the sheep farmer lived
a quiet, simple life. But
when he went down to the
prosperous town of Bethel
to sell his wool, he was
shocked at what he saw there.
The merchants had become rich
and lived well in fine houses.
But Amos could see that they
made their money by swindling
the poor. They also lent money
at high rates of interest. If a
man could not pay his debt, they
seized his land and even sold his family as slaves.

There was no justice for the poor in the courts,
either: judges ruled in favour of the rich.

Even the priests of the temple were as bad. They held
their religious services and offered sacrifices, but their
hearts were made of stone.

Amos shouted to the people of Bethel, "God hates
your evil ways! He will punish you. An enemy will
invade this land and destroy you! You must seek good
and not evil, so that you may survive."

But there was hope for the future. Amos said that
God would not forget his promise to his chosen people,
but would one day restore peace and prosperity to them,
once he had rid them of all their evil ways.

The story of Jonah

Jonah was a prophet who didn't really want to do what God asked of him. When God said, "Go to the city of Nineveh and persuade the people to change their wicked ways," Jonah ran off in the opposite direction and boarded a sailing ship going far away. But God sent a violent storm to toss the ship about. Jonah told the terrified sailors that he had probably made God angry.

"Throw me into the sea," said Jonah, "and the storm will die down." The sailors reluctantly threw Jonah over the side of the ship and immediately the wind dropped.

Then God commanded a big fish to swallow Jonah,

and after three days and nights the big fish spewed him
safely on to a beach. Jonah immediately thanked God for
saving his life. "Now go to Nineveh with my message!"
said God. The people listened to Jonah and were sorry
for their wicked ways, so God forgave them.

Jonah was angry that God should show mercy to
these people. He sat down under a tree and sulked, but
overnight the tree shrivelled up. Jonah felt sorry for it.

God said to him, "Jonah, you feel sorry for this tree
that meant nothing to you. Won't you let me feel sorry
for all the people of Nineveh?" In this way, God showed
that his love was for people of all nations, not just the
people of Israel.

Micah

Micah lived in a small country town in Judah, the southern kingdom. In those days each family had a piece of land to grow their own food. But when the harvest was bad, they had to borrow money to buy food. Moneylenders grew very rich on the extra money they charged for the loan. And if someone could not pay back the loan, then the moneylenders took his land, his house and even sold him and his family as slaves.

Micah was a fiery man, with a fierce love of God. He hated to see the rich growing richer while the poor starved and suffered, and the way the priests and prophets too made money out of the poor and twisted the law to suit themselves. God's commandment was that they should be good to each other.

"God is angry with you!" he told the people of Jerusalem. "He will punish you. Your city will be destroyed." But they did not believe him. They were sure God was in his holy temple and that they would be safe.

"Jerusalem will become a heap of rubble," cried Micah, "and the mountain where the temple stands will become a forest."

The future, however, was hopeful. "From Bethlehem, the smallest of the cities of Judah, will come someone to rule Israel," said Micah. "His origins will lie in the distant past. He will be their shepherd, with the power of the Lord and the majesty of the name of God."

BETHLEHEM

The New Testament

The new covenant

The New Testament (an old word meaning covenant) is all about Jesus: God's own son. He is the one promised to the people through the prophets of the Old Testament: the new covenant between God and his people. It is made up of a number of accounts and letters written by the people who were close to Jesus, or who passed on his teachings after he had left this life on earth.

The coming of the Romans

More than four hundred years passed after the last of the Old Testament prophets promised that God would be sending someone very special to make a new covenant with his people.

They were difficult times.

First, Greek conquerors took over the Promised Land from the Persians.

A hero of the Jewish nation, Judas Maccabeus, fought the Greeks and brought a time of peaceful freedom for a while, but later the Romans conquered the Greeks and Palestine – the Promised Land – came under the Roman rule.

The Roman Empire was huge and powerful. Roman soldiers and officials were put in towns and cities to keep law and order and collect taxes for the Emperor. Everyone hated them. The Jewish people longed for the

day when a new king, or hero, would come and rescue them from Roman rule.

The Romans did not worship the God of the Jewish nation. When a Roman general named Pompey took over the city of Jerusalem, he marched into the temple to see what the Jewish God was like. He expected to see a huge statue, but instead it was quite empty.

The king chosen by the Romans to rule over the people of God at this time was a cruel, clever man called Herod the Great.

A baby for Elizabeth

In the days when Herod was king, there was a priest living in Judaea called Zacharias. He and his wife, Elizabeth, were faithful to God and obedient to his commandments. Their one sorrow was that despite all their prayers, they had not been blessed with children, and now they were both growing old.

One day, while Zacharias was serving in the temple and the people prayed outside, an angel appeared, standing by the altar. Zacharias was terrified.

"Do not be afraid, Zacharias," said the angel. "Your prayers have been heard. Your wife, Elizabeth, is to have a son and you must call him John. He will be a great joy to you both and he will bring a great deal of happiness and peace to the world. He will be great in the eyes of the Lord and through him many people will come back to God."

Zacharias found it hard to believe what the angel was saying to him.

"How can this be?" he asked. "We are old now. My wife is unable to have children."

"I am Gabriel," said the angel. "I come from God with this good news for you. Since you have not believed me, from now on you will be silent until all that I have said comes to pass."

When Zacharias came out of the sanctuary, he could not tell anyone what had happened. The people were amazed: they realised he had seen a vision.

Just as the angel had promised, Elizabeth became pregnant. For five weeks she stayed quietly at home, rejoicing that the Lord God had blessed her in this way.

Mary is chosen

God sent the angel Gabriel to Nazareth, a small town in Galilee. There he appeared to a young woman called Mary, who was engaged to be married to Joseph – a descendant of the family of King David. She was also a cousin of Elizabeth.

"Rejoice, Mary," said Gabriel, "because the Lord is with you. You are the most blessed of all women!"

Mary was very troubled by this. She wondered what the angel's words could mean and why she should have such a special visitor.

"Do not be afraid, Mary," said Gabriel. "You have found favour with God. You will have a son and you must call him Jesus. He will be great. The son of the Most High. He will rule over the people of God and his reign will never end."

"How can this be?" asked Mary. "I am still a girl, and unmarried."

"The Holy Spirit will come to you," said the angel, "and God's power will cover you, so the child will be holy and called the Son of God. Know this as well, that your cousin, Elizabeth, is also going to have a son, even though she is old now. For nothing is impossible to God." Mary knelt down before the angel's feet and bowed her head. "I am God's faithful servant, and prepared to do whatever he asks of me," she said. "Let what you have said be done to me."

And when she looked up, the angel had gone.

Mary visits Elizabeth

After the angel had left, Mary went as quickly as she could to visit her cousin. As soon as Mary entered Zacharias's house and greeted Elizabeth, Elizabeth felt her baby leap for joy inside her womb. Suddenly, Elizabeth was filled with the Holy Spirit.

"Of all women, you are the most blessed!" she cried. "And blessed is the child you carry! As soon as I heard your voice, I felt my baby move inside me. How honoured I am that you have come to visit me."

Mary sang a great song of praise to God:

My soul sings of the greatness of the Lord
and my spirit rejoices in God who is my saviour.

Mary stayed with Elizabeth for three months, and then returned home.

The birth of John the Baptist

Soon afterwards, Elizabeth's baby was born. Just as the angel had promised, it was a boy. All Elizabeth's family and friends shared her happiness.

Now when the time came to give the baby a name, everyone thought he should be called Zacharias, after his father.

"No," said Elizabeth. "His name is John."

"But no one in your family is called John!" they argued. They turned to Zacharias to see what he wanted to call his son. Zacharias was still unable to speak, so he wrote down instead, "His name is John."

At that moment, Zacharias found he was able to speak again, and he gave praise to God.

Baby Jesus

When Joseph discovered that Mary was expecting a child, he decided to quietly release her from her betrothal to him. But an angel came to him in a dream and told him not to be afraid to marry Mary. "The child is from God," said the angel, "and he will be called Jesus."

Now the Romans wanted to know just how many people lived in Palestine, so they could tax them. They ordered every Jewish man to go to his home town to be registered and counted.

When Joseph arrived in his home town of Bethlehem with Mary, it was crowded with people. They had travelled all the way from Nazareth and Mary was very tired. Her baby was due to be born, and they had to find somewhere to rest for the night.

"Sorry, we haven't a room left," said the innkeeper.
"You can go in the stable if you like. There's plenty of
clean straw."

So Joseph made a bed for Mary in the stable, and
that night her son was born. She remembered what the
angel had told her, long before, and called him Jesus.

Mary wrapped baby Jesus in special strips of cloth,
like bandages, called "swaddling". It made him feel very
warm and secure. Jesus was put in one of the food
mangers, where he slept on a bed of straw.

Jesus had been sent by God to save his people. The
saviour they all hoped for was born, not in a royal
palace, but in a stable in Bethlehem.

The shepherds visit Jesus

The night Jesus was born, shepherds on the hillside above Bethlehem were watching over their sheep in the darkness. Suddenly, the sky above them filled with a dazzling light and an angel appeared. The shepherds were terrified. "Don't be afraid," said the angel. "I have great news for you and all people. Today in Bethlehem your saviour has been born. You will find him lying in a manger, in a stable, wrapped in swaddling."

Then the angel was joined by a great choir of angels, singing the praises of God:

Glory to God in the highest heaven,
And peace to those who have pleased him!

When the angels had gone, the shepherds looked at one another in amazement.

"What can this mean?" they said to each other. "Let's go down to Bethlehem and see for ourselves." They hurried down to the town and just as the angel had told them, they found the stable where the new-born baby, wrapped in swaddling, was lying in a manger.

The shepherds were astonished. They told everybody what they had seen and heard, and Mary kept everything they said in her heart.

Then the shepherds returned to their sheep, giving praise and glory to God.

Wise men from the East

After Jesus was born, three wise men came to Jerusalem from the East, guided by a star. They were looking for the promised Messiah. As soon as they had seen the brilliant new star in the sky, they knew that this was the sign they had been waiting for.

"Where is the infant king of the Jews?" they asked everyone. "We have come to worship him. We have followed his star and have gifts for him."

When King Herod heard of the strangers looking for a king, he sent for them and listened to their story, pretending to be as deeply religious as they were and carefully concealing his anger and fear.

"Go to Bethlehem," he told them, "and when you have found the child come and let me know, so that I may go and pay him homage, too."

As the wise men left Jerusalem, the star they had seen appeared before them and led them to Bethlehem, to where Jesus and his parents were staying. They knew they had found the one they were looking for.

They knelt down in front of Jesus and gave him their gifts: gold for a king, frankincense for the worship of God, and myrrh, an oil used when burying the dead.

Afterwards, they returned home a different way. They had been warned in a dream not to go back to Herod, as he only wanted to kill Jesus.

It was the wise men who brought the good news of the Saviour to the world beyond Palestine.

The return to Nazareth

When the wise men had left, Joseph was warned in a dream to take Mary and Jesus to Egypt, where they would be safe from King Herod. The king was furious that the wise men had deceived him. To make sure that there was no rival king to challenge him, Herod ordered his soldiers to kill every young boy under the age of two living in and around Bethlehem.

Not long after this, King Herod died. The angel returned to Joseph in another dream and told him it was safe to return to Israel.

Joseph took Mary and Jesus back home to Nazareth. They made their home there, with a workshop for Joseph's work as a carpenter.

So Jesus grew up, in a loving family devoted to God. Mary would have taught him all about his heavenly father, through the stories and books of the Bible, and the traditional songs of praise and thanksgiving. Joseph would have taken him to the temple for worship and taught him all about making things in wood, so he too could earn his living as a carpenter when he grew up.

As the boy Jesus grew older, he also grew in the knowledge and love of God. Everyone liked him, and God was pleased with him.

Jesus at the temple of Jerusalem

E very year, Joseph, Mary and young Jesus went to Jerusalem to celebrate the feast of the Passover at the temple. It was an exciting, happy, family occasion.

When Jesus was twelve years old, they made the journey as usual, and when the time came to return home, Mary thought Jesus was with friends and relatives in another part of the caravan. By the end of the day, however, it was clear that he was missing. She and Joseph returned to Jerusalem early next morning to look for him.

Three anxious days later, they found Jesus in the temple, talking to the priests and teachers and asking them questions. They were all astonished at how much he knew and understood.

"My child, how could you do this to us?" asked Mary. "We've been searching everywhere for you. We were so worried."

Jesus was surprised. "Why were you looking for me?" he asked. "Didn't you realise I'd be in my father's house, doing his work?" But they didn't understand what he meant. So Jesus went home to Nazareth with them and stayed until it was the right time to start his important work for his heavenly father.

John the Baptist

John was the cousin of Jesus. When John grew up he knew God wanted him to do some very important work for him. He made his home in the desert, wearing clothes made of rough camel hair tied with a leather belt, and living on insects and wild honey. His only companions were the wild creatures of the desert.

Each day John went down to the banks of the River Jordan, where travellers would stop to refresh themselves and their animals, and spoke to them about God.

John was a wild-looking man and his words were stern, fierce and frightening. He warned the people that God was angry with them. He said that they should be

sorry for their evil ways and ask God to forgive them.

News of John spread far and wide. Here was a new prophet; someone sent by God with an important message for them. People flocked from all over the country to hear him preach. John baptised them in the river by dipping them under the water, as a sign that God had forgiven them.

He also told them of the saviour that God was sending. "I am preparing the way for him," said John, "but I am not worthy enough to kneel and untie his sandals. I baptise you with water, but he will baptise you with the spirit of God."

Jesus is baptised

One day, Jesus came to be baptised by John. John knew immediately that this was the promised saviour. "Here is the lamb of God, who will take away the sins of the world!" he said.

Jesus had nothing to be sorry for because he had never disobeyed God, so John asked humbly, "Why do you come to me? It is I who should be baptised by you."

But Jesus said, "I believe this is what God wants."

So John baptised him. When Jesus came up out of the water, the spirit of God in the form of a dove flew down to him and the voice of God said, "This is my beloved son. I am very pleased with him."

"This is the man I spoke about," John said later. "I have seen him and I know he is God's Chosen One."

Not long after this, King Herod – son of the evil King Herod the Great – had John thrown into prison. He did not want to listen to John's message about asking God's forgiveness. Eventually, he had John put to death. Jesus was very sad when he heard the news. "A greater man than John has never lived," he said. "He was the herald, preparing the way for the kingdom of God."

Jesus is tempted

After Jesus had been baptised by John, he was led by the Holy Spirit into the desert to prepare himself, alone, for the tasks ahead. Jesus knew he had an important plan to carry out for his heavenly father, so for many days and nights he prayed to the Father for strength and guidance.

After so long without food, Jesus became exhausted and very hungry. It was then that Satan, the enemy of God, came to him.

"If you are really the Son of God," said Satan, "why don't you turn this stone into a loaf of bread and stop feeling hungry?"

But Jesus refused to use the power God had given him to satisfy his own need. "The Bible teaches us that we cannot live on just bread," Jesus told Satan. "We need the word of God as well."

Then Satan took Jesus to a high place and
showed him the whole world. "All this can be yours,"
he said, "if you will kneel and worship me!"

Jesus replied, "The first Commandment is that we
should worship the Lord our God and serve him alone."

Finally Satan took Jesus to the top of the temple in
Jerusalem. "If you are the Son of God," he said, "throw
yourself off this temple. The Bible says that God's angels
will make sure you are not hurt!"

Jesus replied, "It also says that you must not put the
Lord your God to the test!"

And with that, Satan left.

God sent his angels to help Jesus after his ordeal, and
give him food to eat.

Jesus visits Nazareth

Jesus left the desert and went down into Galilee, where he started to tell people all about God and how they should live their lives in order to please him.

One day he went into Nazareth, the town where he had grown up and worked as a carpenter.

It was the Sabbath, the holy day of the week, and he went to the synagogue with the other Jewish men. During the service, Jesus stood up to read and he was given the scroll of the prophet Isaiah. He opened it and read a passage which told of the coming of the Messiah, or Saviour.

Then Jesus said, "Today, these words have come true. God has sent me to bring you the good news of his kingdom."

At first everyone listened to him. Jesus spoke well, and they were astonished at the things he was saying to them. Then gradually they began to whisper to each other, "This is the carpenter's son, isn't it? Who does he think he is? How can he say such things!"

"A prophet is never believed by his own people," Jesus said to them.

The crowd became angry then, and they seized Jesus, intending to do him harm. Jesus, however, managed to slip away to safety. He never went back to Nazareth. Instead he went to other towns and villages, telling the Good News about God's kingdom, and healing people who were sick.

Jesus calls fishermen

Jesus needed friends to help him with his work. As he walked down by the Sea of Galilee, he saw some fishermen casting their net into the water to catch fish. They were brothers: Simon and Andrew.

Jesus called to them and they came back to the shore.

"Follow me," said Jesus, "and I will make you fishers of people." At once, the two men left their nets and joined him, for they knew Jesus was the promised Messiah.

A little further on, Jesus came to the brothers James and John. They were in their father's fishing boat, mending the nets with their father, Zebedee.

When Jesus called to them, they immediately left the boat and their father and followed him. They, too, knew that Jesus was sent by God.

Jesus chose these men not because they were clever or gifted, but because he knew they were strong, honest and loyal to God. He would later give Simon a new name: Peter, which means "rock". And James and John he called the "sons of thunder" because they were keen, fiery young men.

Instead of gathering fish into their nets, Peter, Andrew, James and John would gather people into the kingdom of God.

These four disciples stayed close to Jesus always, learning from him and helping him as he travelled the country, teaching and healing.

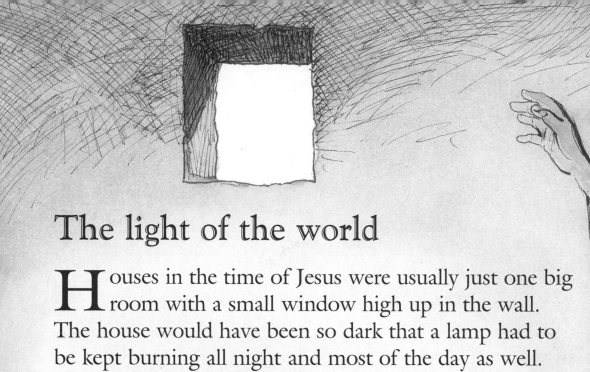

The light of the world

Houses in the time of Jesus were usually just one big room with a small window high up in the wall. The house would have been so dark that a lamp had to be kept burning all night and most of the day as well.

Lamps were made of clay, with a handle for carrying. There was one hole for the wick – made of flax – and another hole for pouring in the olive oil.

Jesus said to his followers, "When you light a lamp, you don't put it under the bed, or under a basin, do you? Of course not. You put it on a table where it can light up the whole house. You must be like that lamp. Let your light shine out for everyone so that they can see the love and goodness of God shining in everything you do. Be a good example for them. They will see that your light comes from God and will give him thanks and praise."

Jesus taught his followers all about the kingdom of God, and he was the perfect example of love and obedience to his heavenly father. The apostle, John, wrote that Jesus was "The light of men, a light that shines in the dark, a light that darkness could not overpower."

And Jesus himself said, "I am the light of the world. Whoever follows me will not be walking in the dark; he will have the light of life."

So when Jesus sent his disciples out to be the Light of the World, they knew exactly what he meant.

Jesus teaches about prayer

Jesus often went off by himself to pray. One day, when he returned from one of these sessions, the disciples asked him to teach them how they should pray.

"When you pray," said Jesus, "don't pray in the open, where everyone will see you. Instead, go to your room and shut the door. God sees and hears everything, and he will hear your prayer. Talk directly to God, like this:

Our Father in heaven,
may your name be held holy,
your kingdom come to us,
your will be done on earth,
as it is in heaven.
Give us today our daily bread
and forgive us our sins,
as we forgive the sins of others.
Do not test us, but keep us safe
from evil.

"Ask in prayer, and it will be given to you. Search for God, and you will find him. Knock, and he will open the door to you. Those who ask will receive, those who seek will find, and the door is opened for the person who knocks.

"What caring father would give his son a stone when he asks for bread? Or would give him a snake when he asks for fish? If you who are weak know what is good for your children, how much more will your heavenly father give good things to those who ask him."

The kingdom of heaven

Jesus taught that finding the kingdom of God is like finding a hidden treasure.

In those days it was usual for people to bury their money in the ground. They felt it was safe there, for only the person who dug the hole knew where it was. However, if the person died or went away, then his money might lie in the ground undiscovered for years and years. The law said that if anyone found buried treasure like this on his land, he could keep it.

One day a man was walking across a field when he stumbled against something hard in the ground. He scraped away the earth and discovered a box, full of treasure.

Delighted, he quickly covered up the box again and hurried into town to buy the field. He had to sell everything to raise the money he needed, but then the field – and the treasure – was his!

"The kingdom of heaven," said Jesus, "is also like a pearl merchant finding a pearl of great value. He sells all his other, inferior pearls in order to buy it."

A person will come across the kingdom by chance, but as soon as they have found it they will realise that it is the greatest treasure of all, and they will give up everything to possess it.

"It's like a net thown into the sea," Jesus went on. "It catches all kinds of creatures. When it's full it is hauled to shore and emptied. The good fish are kept but the useless creatures arc thrown away.

So, when the world comes to an end the angels will separate the good from the bad. The good will be taken into heaven, but the bad will be tossed into eternal fire."

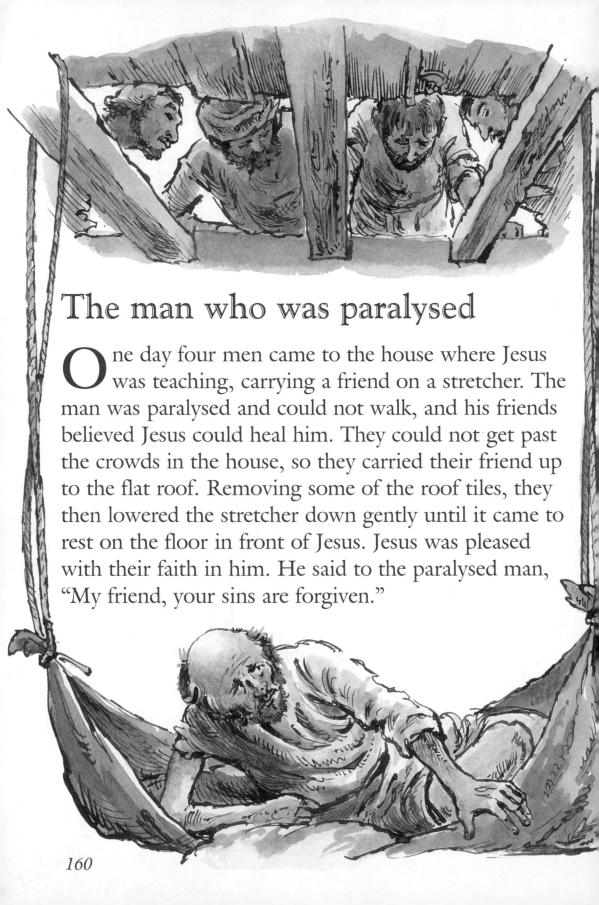

The man who was paralysed

One day four men came to the house where Jesus was teaching, carrying a friend on a stretcher. The man was paralysed and could not walk, and his friends believed Jesus could heal him. They could not get past the crowds in the house, so they carried their friend up to the flat roof. Removing some of the roof tiles, they then lowered the stretcher down gently until it came to rest on the floor in front of Jesus. Jesus was pleased with their faith in him. He said to the paralysed man, "My friend, your sins are forgiven."

This made some of the people in the crowd very angry. "Only God can forgive sins," they said.

Jesus knew what they were saying. "Which is easier?" he asked them. "To say to this man, 'Your sins are forgiven,' or 'Get up and walk.'? To prove to you that I am the Son of God and able to forgive sins, I say to this man, 'Get up, pick up your stretcher and go home!'"

To the shock and amazement of everyone in the room, the man got up from his stretcher, rolled it up and walked away.

They all praised God. "We've never seen anything like this before!" they said.

Jesus calls a tax collector

Matthew was a tax collector in the town of Capernaum. It was his job to collect taxes for the Romans from the people of the town, as well as the many traders and fishermen that brought goods by sea into the busy port.

Everyone hated the Romans who had conquered Palestine, and they hated even more the men who collected taxes for them. Often the tax collectors charged more than was needed and kept the extra for themselves.

As Jesus went by the customs house he saw Matthew sitting at the table, counting his money, and called to him. "Come, Matthew. Follow me."

Without a second thought, Matthew immediately left everything to follow this man he had heard so much about.

That night, Matthew gave a party at his house in honour of Jesus, his new friend. He invited all his other friends – many of them hated tax collectors like himself – so they could meet Jesus, too. When the officials at the temple heard of the party, they complained to Jesus, "Why do you sit at the same table, eating and drinking with such evil men?"

But Jesus told them, "People who are well do not need a doctor. I have not come to help people who already love and serve God. I have come to help those who are in need of God's forgiveness."

The centurion's servant

At Capernaum there lived a Roman centurion – an army officer in charge of a hundred soldiers. His servant was very ill and dying. The centurion had heard about Jesus, so he asked some of the Jewish elders to go to Jesus and ask him for his help.

As Jesus approached the town, the elders came to him and told him about the centurion. "He is a good man," they said, "and worthy of your help. He built the synagogue for us and has been very kind to our people."

Jesus agreed to go and see him. But before he reached the centurion's house, however, some of the centurion's friends came to meet him with a message.

They told him that the centurion had said: "Sir, do not put yourself to any trouble for me, I am not worthy for you to enter my house, and for this reason I did not come to you myself. Please just say the word and my servant will be healed. For, like you, I am a person who has authority: I only have to say to one of my soldiers, 'Go!' and he goes, or to another, 'Come here!' and he comes."

When Jesus heard the centurion's message, he was astonished. He turned to the crowd of people following him and said, "Not in the whole of Israel have I come across faith such as this."

The messengers returned to the centurion's house and found his servant completely healed.

A woman in the crowd

There was always a crowd of people around Jesus wherever he went. Some wanted to be healed by him, or ask him to heal someone for them.

One day there was a woman in the crowd who had been ill for many years. She had spent all her money paying doctors to cure her, but their treatments had not helped her. In fact, she was getting worse.

She believed in Jesus and his wonderful powers of healing, and was determined to get close to him. "If I can just touch his clothes," she thought, "I know I will

be well again." At last she touched the hem of Jesus' cloak and she knew at once that she had been cured.

Suddenly, Jesus stopped. He knew power had gone out of him. "Who touched my cloak?" he asked.

The disciples were astonished. "With all these people pressing round you, how can you ask that question?"

But Jesus continued to look all round the crowd. Then the woman came forward, fell at his feet trembling with fear, and admitted what she had done.

"My daughter," said Jesus kindly, "your faith has healed you. Go in peace and be free of your illness."

The daughter of Jairus

O ne day, Jairus, who was the head of the
synagogue – the Jewish place of worship –
pushed through the crowd and fell at Jesus' feet,
weeping. "Master," he cried, "my only daughter is
dying. Please come, I know you can save her."

"I'll come at once," said Jesus. But on the way he
stopped to help a woman who had been ill for many
years. As they went on to Jairus' house, Jesus and Jairus
were met by one of Jairus' servants. "It's too late," he
said to Jairus. "Your daughter is dead."

"Don't worry," said Jesus. "Just have faith and she
will be safe."

When they arrived at the house, Jesus sent away all the weeping mourners. "The child is not dead," he told them. "She's just asleep." But they only laughed at him.

Jesus went in to the little girl and took her hand. "Come! Get up!" he said to her. The girl opened her eyes. Then she sat up.

"She is hungry," said Jesus to the girl's astonished parents. "You must give her something to eat. But don't tell anyone about what has happened here today."

The miracle of the loaves and fishes

Jesus sent his twelve disciples out into the countryside in pairs, to continue his work of teaching and healing among the people. When they returned, he could see they were very tired and needed to rest. So they set off by boat, heading for a quiet place near Bethsaida where they could be by themselves.

However, some people saw them leave and guessed where they were going. Before long, people from all the towns and villages around were hurrying to get there ahead of them. When Jesus stepped ashore, he could see a huge crowd waiting for him and he felt sorry for them. "They are like sheep without a shepherd," he said. And he talked to them and taught them for some time.

As the day drew to a close, the disciples came up to Jesus. "It's getting late," they said. "You should send these people to the villages, away from this lonely place, so they can get food."

"Give them something to eat yourselves," said Jesus.

They were shocked. "What? Are we to spend a fortune on bread for them all?"

"How many loaves do you have?" asked Jesus. "And how many fish? Go and see."

They reported that they had five loaves and two fish.

Jesus told them to gather the people together in groups. He took the loaves and fish and looked up to heaven and gave thanks. Then he handed them to his disciples and instructed them to share them out among the people. There were over five thousand people in the crowd: everyone ate as much as they wanted, and still there were twelve baskets of scraps left over.

Jesus walks on the water

Jesus sent his disciples off in the boat while he sent the crowds away. He promised to join them at Bethsaida, but in the meantime he went off by himself to pray.

By evening, the boat was far out on the Sea of Galilee. There were strong winds blowing, and very soon the disciples were worn out trying to row against them.

Jesus knew that they were in trouble, so he walked across the surface of the sea towards them.

When the disciples saw him approaching, they were terrified. "It is a ghost!" they cried.

"Take courage!" said Jesus. "It is I. Do not be afraid."

Peter then said, "Lord, if it is really you, then tell me to come to you across the water."

"Come!" said Jesus, holding out his hands.

Peter cautiously stepped out of the boat and put his feet on the water. He took a few steps towards Jesus and sure enough he, too, was able to walk on the surface of the sea. It felt marvellous! But suddenly Peter felt the strength of the wind against him, and he became afraid. Then he started to sink.

"Help me, Lord!" he cried. "I'm sinking!"

Jesus put out his hand at once and held him. "Oh, Peter!" he said. "Why did you doubt? You have such little faith."

As they both got into the boat, the wind dropped. The others in the boat were stunned at what they had seen. "Truly," they said, "you arc the Son of God."

The good neighbour

O ne day a lawyer asked Jesus to explain the
Commandment, *Love your neighbour as yourself.*
"Who is my neighbour?" he asked. Jesus told this story:

A man was travelling from Jerusalem to Jericho,
when he was attacked by a gang of robbers. They took
his money and clothes, and left him to die. A priest and
a Levite – a servant at the temple – both came along the
road, but hurried by on the other side without stopping.

Later, a Samaritan traveller came along. (Samaritans
were considered to be the enemies of the people of God.)

He saw the injured man and went to him. He bandaged
the man's wounds and covered him with his own cloak.
Then he lifted the man onto his donkey and took him to
an inn, where he hired a room and looked after him.

The next day the Samaritan gave two silver coins to
the innkeeper. "Take care of this man," he said. "If you
spend more than that I'll repay you on my way back."

Jesus asked the lawyer, "Which of these three do you
think was a good neighbour to the injured man?"

"The one who was kind to him," the lawyer replied.

"That's right," said Jesus. "Then go and be a good
neighbour, just like him."

Jesus heals
a blind man

One day Jesus and his disciples came to the town of Bethsaida. There, some people brought a blind man to him. "Please put your hands on him and heal him, master," they said to Jesus.

Jesus took the man by the hand and led him out of the town, away from the crowds. When they were alone, Jesus anointed the man's eyes and laid his hands on him.

"Can you see anything yet?" Jesus asked him.

"Yes!" said the man, getting excited. "I can see trees! But they are walking around – so they must be people!"

Jesus laid his hands on the man's eyes again and he was cured.

"I can see!" cried the man joyfully. "Now I can see everything!"

Jesus said to him, "Go back home, now. Don't go into the town and don't speak of this to anyone."

The lost sheep

Jesus also used stories, or parables, to explain God's love for everyone. He often compared God to a shepherd looking after his sheep. One parable he told was this:

There was once a shepherd with a flock of a hundred sheep. Every morning the shepherd led them to places where the grass was good to eat, and every evening led them back down to the safety of the stone fold.

As the sheep entered the sheepfold, the shepherd counted them to make sure they were all there. One evening he only counted ninety-nine sheep. One was missing!

Immediately, the shepherd left the ninety-nine sheep in the sheepfold and went back up the hillside to search for the one that was lost. For hours he searched. Then, when he found the frightened lamb, he put it across his shoulders and carried it joyfully all the way back to the sheepfold.

When the shepherd finally got home, he was so happy that he called all his family and friends round for a party. "Come and celebrate with me!" he told them. "I have found my lamb that was lost!"

In the same way, Jesus explained, God loves each one of us so much that he rejoices more over one person who comes back to him, than over all the people already safe in his care.

The lost coin

Jesus told a story about a woman who wore ten silver coins on her headdress, to explain God's love for us. In those days it was usual for women to wear their money like jewellery in this way: they would punch a hole in each coin and sew them to the veil they wore on their head. It kept their money safe and showed everyone how well off they were!

One day, the woman in the story was horrified to see that one coin had fallen off. She would have to search the whole house until she found it!

She lit a lamp to help her with the search, and then she began to sweep every corner of the room carefully, moving all the furniture to make sure nothing was overlooked. Suddenly, she saw the coin glinting in the dust and picked it up!

She was so happy that she ran out into the street and shouted across to her friends and neighbours, "Come and share my joy! I lost one of my coins this morning, but now I've found it!"

Everyone was delighted for her. They knew just what it was like to lose something precious.

It is just like that with God, Jesus said. We are all precious to him, and he is overjoyed whenever one person who was "lost" turns back to him and asks for his forgiveness.

The lost son

There was once a rich farmer who had two sons. He loved them both and planned to share his estate out equally between them when he died.

The younger son decided he didn't want to wait that long. So he went to his father and asked him if he could have his share of the money now, while he was young enough to enjoy it.

The father was sad, but he did as his son asked because he loved him.

The son then went to live in a foreign city, where he had a wonderful time and made many new friends. But before long his money was spent and his friends left him.

In desperation, the son took on a job with a local farmer, feeding his pigs. There were times when he would have gladly eaten the pig food, he was so hungry. Then he realised how silly he was being.

"Here I am dying of hunger," he said to himself, "when even my father's hired servants have more food than they need! I will go back home and say to my father: 'Father, I have behaved badly. I am not fit to be called your son. Please give me a job on your farm!'"

But while he was still a long way off, his father saw him coming and ran to meet him. The son tried to say the words he had practised, but his father took no notice. Instead he hugged him tightly and called to the servants, "Quick! Bring fine clothes! Prepare a feast! My son was lost – and now he's found!"

The lost son and his brother

Jesus continued telling the story of the lost son who returned home like this: As the farmer's older son made his way home after a hard day working in the fields, he heard the sounds of music and dancing coming from the farmhouse. He called one of the servants. "What's going on?" he asked. "What are all the celebrations for?"

"Your brother has come home," replied the servant, "and your father's having a party for him because he is so happy to have him back safe and sound."

The older brother was so angry he would not go inside the farmhouse. Eventually, his father came out to plead with his son to come indoors.

But the son only shouted at his father. "I've slaved for you all these years!" he said crossly. "And not once have you ever had a party for me or my friends. But the minute this lazy, good-for-nothing boy of yours comes back after wasting all your money, you bring out the best food and drink and treat him to all this."

"My dear son," the father said gently, "you are always with me and I love you for it. Everything I have is yours. But it was only right that we should celebrate because your brother here was lost and now he's found again."

The younger son was selfish and greedy, while the older son was jealous and bitter. Even so, the father loved them. In the same way, Jesus explained, God loves us and is always ready to receive those who ask for his forgiveness.

Jesus is transfigured

Jesus asked his disciples, "Who do people say I am?"
"Some say you are John the Baptist," they said.
"Some say you are Elijah, or one of the other prophets."

But Jesus asked them. "Who do you think I am?"

"You are the Christ," said Simon Peter. "The son of the living God."

"You are a happy man, Simon," said Jesus, "for only my heavenly father could have told you this. From now on you will be called Peter and you will be the rock on which I shall build my church. I will give you the keys of the kingdom of heaven." The name Peter meant "rock".

A few days later, Jesus took Peter, James and John up a high mountain, to pray. Suddenly, Jesus was transfigured in front of them: his face shone like the sun and his clothes became dazzlingly white. Moses and Elijah appeared by his side and talked to him. Then a bright cloud covered them all and a voice came from heaven saying, "This is my beloved son, with whom I am well pleased. Listen to him."

The disciples were terrified and hid their faces. When they looked up again, they saw only Jesus standing there.

Jesus touched them. "Come, stand up," he said quietly. "Do not be afraid."

As they came down from the mountain, Jesus ordered them, "Do not tell anyone about what you have seen, until I have risen from death."

But the disciples did not know what he meant.

Jesus the friend of children

Jesus showed that God's love was for all people. He was a friend to everyone – especially those who were poor, or sick or unimportant – and particularly children.

One day, the disciples asked Jesus, "Who is the greatest in the kingdom of heaven?"

Jesus knew that they were really asking about how they could become powerful themselves. Before he answered their question, Jesus called over a little boy who was playing in front of them, sat him on his knee and put his arms round him.

"You see this child?" he asked them. "Well, unless your hearts change and you become as obedient and trusting as this little child, you will not be able to enter the kingdom of heaven.

"Anyone who welcomes children in my name, welcomes me," said Jesus. "But make sure you never treat children badly, because their angels in heaven are always close to God, looking after them."

People often brought their children to Jesus, so he could lay his hands on them and say a prayer. His friends tried to send them away, but Jesus said, "Do not stop the children coming to me. It is to children like these that the kingdom of heaven belongs."

Using our talents

Jesus also described the kingdom of heaven in another story: a rich man going on a long journey divided his money between his servants, according to their abilities. To one he gave five measures of gold, or talents, to another he gave two, and to a third, one.

The first two servants traded with their gold and were able to double what they had been given, but the third buried his one talent safely in the ground.

Their master returned and sent for them. "Sir," said the first, "I have made five more talents for you."

"And I have made you two more," said the second.

"Well done!" said the rich man. "You have both been faithful in small things so I shall put you in charge of greater things. I am very pleased."

But the third servant said, "I was afraid I would lose your money so I hid it safely in the ground."

His master was furious. "If you were worried about losing my money," he cried, "you should have put it in the bank to earn interest for me." And he ordered the servant to be thrown out of the house.

God gives each of us different gifts, or talents, and he wants us to use them well if we are to serve him and enter his kingdom.

Jesus at Bethany

The feast of the Passover was drawing near. Jesus and his disciples journeyed to Jerusalem and stopped at the village of Bethany, at the house of some friends, the sisters Martha and Mary, and their brother Lazarus, whom Jesus had earlier restored to life.

That evening they sat down to dinner, which Martha served for them. During the meal, Mary came in with a jar of very expensive perfumed oil. Kneeling at Jesus' feet, she poured the oil over them, wiping it away with her hair. The air was scented with the fragrance of the oil.

"What a waste! That oil should have been sold and the money given to the poor!" said Judas Iscariot, the disciple who looked after their common fund of money. He didn't say this because he cared for the poor, but because he was a thief and often helped himself from the fund.

"Leave her alone," said Jesus. "When she anointed my feet, she was preparing me for burial. There will always be poor people, but I shall not always be with you."

Judas was so angry that he left the house and went straight to the chief priests of the temple to see how he might betray Jesus to them.

Jesus enters Jerusalem

On the first day of the Passover week Jesus sent two of his disciples ahead of him, to the village of Bethphage. "You will find a young donkey there, tied up with its mother. Untie it and bring it back with you. If you are asked what you are doing, just say 'the Master needs it and will send it back soon.'"

The disciples found everything just as Jesus had said. They brought the donkey back to Jesus and covered it with their coats to make a saddle. It had never been ridden before, but it willingly allowed Jesus to sit on its back.

And so Jesus travelled into the great city of Jerusalem, not riding the war-horse of a king, but on the back of a donkey, just as the prophet Zechariah had foretold long before. The promised Messiah was a king of peace, not war.

Crowds of people rushed into the streets to see Jesus and welcome him. They spread their cloaks on the ground in front of him and shouted "Hosannah!", joyfully praising God and singing, "Blessed is he who comes in the name of the Lord!"

But there was a group of religious men in the crowd, called Pharisees. They did not approve of all the noise and excitement at this holy time, or the way Jesus was so popular with everyone. It only made them want to get rid of him all the more.

As he came in sight of the holy city itself, Jesus became very sad and wept. He knew that Jerusalem would not listen to his message of peace, and would one day be destroyed.

The last supper

It was the feast of Passover, and Jesus knew he would
soon die and return to his father in heaven. During
their last supper together, Jesus warned his disciples that
one of them would betray him. "I tell you," said Jesus, "it
would be better for that man if he had never been born."

Then Jesus took some of the bread they were going
to eat and blessed it. He broke the bread and handed it
to his disciples. "Take this and eat. This is my body."
Then he took a cup of wine and gave thanks. "This is
my blood, the new covenant," he said, "which shall be
poured out for many so that their sins will be forgiven."

He passed the cup round for them all to drink. "From now on," Jesus told them, "I shall not drink wine with you again until I share the new wine with you in the kingdom of my father."

After supper Jesus took his disciples out of the city. As they walked he told them, "You will all lose faith tonight and desert me."

Peter protested, saying, "Even if everyone else loses faith, I won't!"

But Jesus answered him, "Before the cock crows twice tonight, you will disown me three times."

The garden of Gethsemane

Jesus and his disciples came to a quiet garden of olive trees, called Gethsemane.

There he asked his disciples to wait for him while he took his three closest friends, Peter, James and John, to a lonely part of the garden to pray. He became very troubled and deeply distressed. "My soul is full of sorrow," he told them. "Wait here for me and stay awake."

Jesus went further into the garden and threw himself on the ground, "Father," he prayed, "everything is possible for you. Take this suffering away from me.

But let it be as your will, not mine, would be done."

His friends were so tired, they could not keep their eyes open. Twice Jesus returned to them to find them asleep. The third time he said, "It is all over. Come, get up. My betrayer is here."

Just then Judas Iscariot came up to him, followed by a band of men armed with clubs and swords sent by the chief priests. He greeted Jesus with a kiss: this was the signal for the armed men to seize Jesus.

Terrified, the disciples all ran away.

The death of Jesus

Even though the chief priests paid people to lie about Jesus, they were unable to pass the death sentence on him: only the Roman governor could do that. So they decided to take him to Pontius Pilate.

Meanwhile, Peter waited outside in the courtyard to see what would happen. A serving-girl and others saw him and accused Peter of being one of the followers of Jesus. Three times Peter denied it. And then a cock crowed and Peter remembered what Jesus had said to him. He wept with shame and sorrow.

When Jesus was brought before Pilate, the governor could see that Jesus was not a criminal. But he was afraid of upsetting the Jewish leaders. It was the custom for one prisoner to be released at festival time, so Pilate asked them, "Would you like me to release this Jesus of Nazareth for you?"

"No!" they shouted. "Crucify him!"

Pilate released a murderer called Barabbas instead, and handed Jesus over to be put to death on a cross.

Jesus was mocked by the Roman soldiers, beaten with whips and made to carry his cross through the city to the place of execution. He was so weak that the soldiers had to force a man called Simon of Cyrene to help him. Finally, Jesus was nailed to the cross, between two thieves who had been crucified with him. Darkness covered the land. The moment Jesus died, the curtain in the great temple tore in two from top to bottom.

Mary in the garden

Joseph of Arimathea, a secret disciple of Jesus, asked Pilate for permission to bury the body of Jesus before the Sabbath day began at sunset. Joseph was helped by his friend, Nicodemus. They wrapped the body and laid it in a new tomb cut out of rock. Then they rolled a huge stone in front of the entrance and went home.

As soon as the Sabbath was over, Mary Magdalene and another woman came to the tomb. To their astonishment, they saw the stone had been rolled back from the entrance. The tomb was empty. The women ran to tell the disciples what they had found, and Peter and one of the others came to see for themselves. Afterwards, Mary stayed in the garden, weeping. Someone spoke to her, asking, "Woman, why are you crying?"

"They have taken my Lord," she sobbed, "and I don't know where they have put him." She thought she was talking to one of the gardeners. "Sir, if you have taken him away, tell me where he is so I can give him a proper burial."

"Mary!" said the stranger, softly.

Suddenly, Mary knew that voice. "Master!" she cried, joyfully, and she threw herself at Jesus.

"Do not cling to me," he said to her, "but go and tell my friends that you have seen me."

In the upper room

Later that day, the disciples met together in the room where they had eaten their last supper with Jesus. The door was locked, because they were afraid of what might happen to them if the Jewish leaders found them.

Suddenly, Jesus was there with them.

"Peace be with you," he said. "Why are you so afraid? See my hands and feet. It's really me!" The disciples were speechless with joy.

Jesus told them he was going to send them out to do his work, just as the Father had sent him. They were to stay hidden until he could send the Holy Spirit to them.

One of the disciples, Thomas, had not been in the room at the time. When the others told him Jesus had

actually appeared to them, he did not believe them. "I won't believe until I have seen and touched him for myself," he said.

A few days later, Jesus came again to the room where the disciples were staying. The door was still locked. This time Thomas was with them.

"Peace be with you!" said Jesus, and he turned to Thomas. "See my hands, Thomas. Here, touch my side and believe in me."

Thomas fell to his knees. "My Lord and my God!" he cried.

"You believe because you can see me," said Jesus. "Happy and blessed are those who cannot see me yet believe in me."

The Ascension

Jesus appeared to his disciples for the last time on the Mount of Olives. "Go and tell the whole world the Good News," he told them. "I shall be with you always, to the end of time." Then he was lifted up and a cloud carried him out of sight, into heaven. The disciples returned to Jerusalem and saw Jesus no more.

They were all gathered together in the upper room, when the sound of a rushing wind filled the house. Then flames appeared, which separated and came to rest on the head of each one. They were filled with the Holy Spirit and immediately began to speak in foreign languages.

Visitors from many different countries were astonished that they could understand what these men from Galilee were saying. They were deeply moved by Peter's words: "God raised Jesus to life," he told them, "and all of us are witnesses. He is the promised Lord and Saviour."

"What must we do?" they asked.

"You must change your hearts," said Peter, "and be baptised in the name of Jesus. Then your sins will be forgiven and you will receive the Holy Spirit."

That day three thousand people were baptised and gave their hearts and lives to Jesus. It was the birthday of the new church – the new people of God.

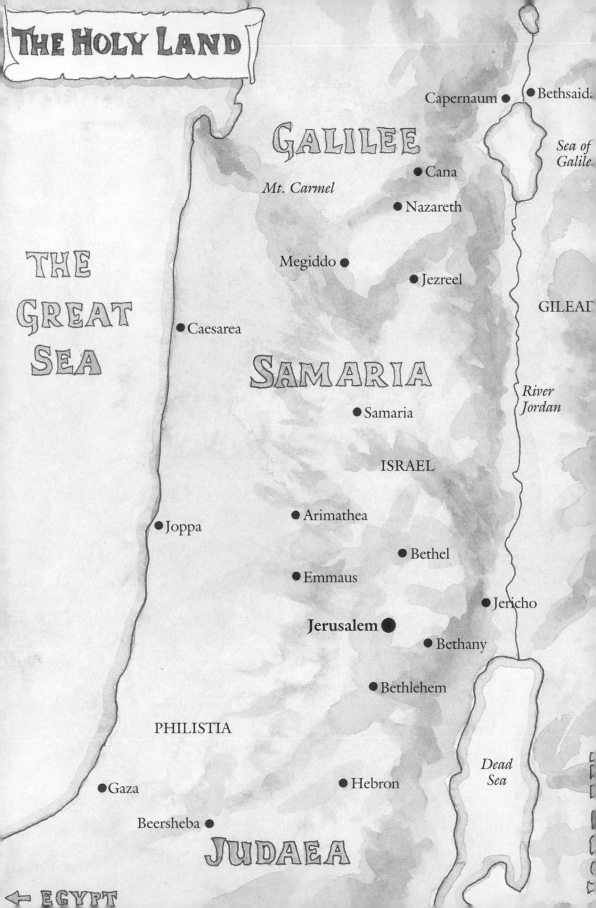